Contents

Acknowledgements

The authors and publishers wish to thank the following for permission to reproduce copyright material on the pages indicated:

Barry Rose for the extract from *The Hammersmith Teenage Project* (NACRO) (pp. 75-6).

Group Analysis for the extract from B. Truckle and E. Schardt, 'Notes on a Counselling Group for Adolescents' in issue no. VIII/3 (p. 57).

Jonathan Cape for the extracts from E. de Bono, *The Use of Lateral Thinking* (pp. 108-10).

Routledge & Kegan Paul for the extract from M. Davies, *Support Systems in Social Work* (p. 41).

Social Work Today for the extract from R. L. James, 'Management by Objectives' in issue no. 6.21 (p. 113).

Youth in Society (the bi-monthly interprofessional journal for everyone concerned with young people) for the extract from S. Millham, 'I.T.? Symbol or Solution; Part 1: I.T. and the Residential Tradition' in issue no. 26 (National Youth Bureau, 17-23 Albion Street, Leicester, LE1 6GD) (p. 80).

The authors also wish to acknowledge their indebtedness to T. Douglas, *Groupwork Practice* (Tavistock Publications), and to thank Tony Scott of the National Institute for Social Work for Table 6.2 (p. 114).

COMMUNITY CARE PRACTICE HANDBOOKS

General Editor: **Martin Davies**

Intermediate Treatment and Social Work

COMMUNITY CARE PRACTICE HANDBOOKS
General Editor: Martin Davies

Intermediate Treatment and Social Work

Ray Jones
Lecturer in Social Work,
University of Bath

Andrew Kerslake
Tutor in Social Work,
University of Bath

HEINEMANN EDUCATIONAL BOOKS
LONDON

Heinemann Educational Books Ltd
22 Bedford Square, London WC1B 3HH
LONDON EDINBURGH MELBOURNE AUCKLAND
HONG KONG SINGAPORE KUALA LUMPUR NEW DELHI
IBADAN NAIROBI JOHANNESBURG
EXETER (NH) KINGSTON PORT OF SPAIN

364·6 JON

British Library Cataloguing in Publication Data
Jones, Ray
  Intermediate treatment and social work.
  — (Community care practice handbooks; no.3).
  1. Juvenile delinquency — Great Britain
  2. Social work with delinquents and criminals
  — Great Britain
  I. Title   II. Kerslake, Andrew
  III. Series
  364.6   HV9145.A5
  ISBN 0-435-82483-X

Typeset by The Castlefield Press of High Wycombe
in 10/12 pt Press Roman, and printed in Great Britain by
Spottiswoode Ballantyne Ltd., Colchester and London

1. What Is Intermediate Treatment?

> These are the new flexible kinds of supervision which I and my
> advisers believe can bring a new – I was going to say 'excitement' –
> into the way in which we treat young people to help them to grow
> up into mature citizens.

This is how James Callaghan, the then Home Secretary, described intermediate treatment when presenting the second reading of the Children
and Young Persons Bill in 1969. This Bill was the culmination of a wide-
ranging debate in the 1960s when delinquency moved into the centre of
the stage of political drama. Three White Papers, a report by a Labour
Party study group, and a booklet by the Fabian Society provided much
of the script for this drama . . . and one of the conclusions to the plot
was the advent of 'intermediate treatment'.

This book explores what is meant by 'intermediate treatment' (IT),
how it may be implemented as a social policy, and how it may be prac-
tised as a range of techniques and services for young people – especially
young people 'in trouble'. The intention is to offer some practical guide-
lines and examples which may help to clarify what has become a rather
confusing term – 'IT'. But in trying to understand what is meant by
intermediate treatment we need to start by locating IT in its historical
and social context.

The Golden Era of the 1960s

Intermediate treatment is a reflection of the social and political concerns
and changes of the 1960s. The sixties saw a growing awareness of deprivation and disadvantage; the Welfare State was no longer seen to have
provided a panacea for all our social ills and difficulties. The post-war
euphoria of the 1950s, when those who had difficulties were felt to
manufacture them for themselves (the 'work-shy', the 'problem families',
the 'inadequates'), was eclipsed by an awareness of poverty and of inequal-
ity at a time when many had 'never had it so good'. There was an ideological bud-burst, this was the time of flower-power and hippies, of love, peace,

and freedom. Man was seen as being restricted by his social and cultural environment. The answer was to 'do your own thing'.

At the same time as these libertarian sentiments were popular among middle-class youth, there was also a growing political interest by many young people. Campaigns against the Vietnam War, the riots of 1968 in Paris, the proliferation of pressure groups (C.P.A.G., Shelter, Gingerbread), and the popularity of left-wing movements among students, all reflected this upsurge in political interest and activity among middle-class young people. By contrast, the sixties was also a time for the emergence (and demise) of many working-class youth styles – the mods and rockers, the crombies, the skinheads. It was these groups which became the focus of the moral panic about delinquency.

All this is of relevance to intermediate treatment in three ways. First, delinquency was a major media and political concern in the 1960s; something 'had to be done about it'. But secondly, what was to be done reflects the changing social values of the sixties. These are highlighted in the 1969 Children and Young Persons Act. The child was seen as deprived rather than depraved; as the victim of his social environment rather than as the destroyer of it. Thirdly, the changing social context of the sixties was the one in which many of the young people who were to become social workers were socialized.

Prior to the end of the 1960s social work was a relatively small concern. There were only, for instance, about 3,000 child care officers in 1969. This was recognized as a major issue in the debate about the Children and Young Persons Bill (Hansard, 1969). The Home Secretary announced a training programme aiming at 'an output of about 1,100 students a year'. Another M.P., in supporting the Bill, stated that 'this is a field which should attract a great many young people who are genuinely concerned about social problems and who perhaps give vent to their concern in ways which are not always regarded as desirable by authority. Their genuine concern could well be channelled into this work.' Hence working with and for children, especially children in trouble, was seen as one employment opportunity for the socially concerned young person in the late 1960s. The work that needed to be undertaken was phrased in terms of care rather than control, and of treatment rather than punishment. The aim was to counter deprivation, and the assumption was that this would reduce delinquency; there was little mention of deterrence and retribution. The ideology of middle-class, educated youth was accommodated within changing social policy for young offenders.

Social Policy and Intermediate Treatment

But what was the policy-making process which led to this accommodation? This process can most immediately be traced back to the early sixties, when the Ingleby Committee reported in 1960 on social work services for children. It emphasized preventive work in the community with the aim of avoiding delinquency and the need to receive children into care. This report led to the 1963 Children and Young Persons Act, with its emphasis in section 1 on *promoting* the welfare of children by helping them, and their families, *in the community*.

This trend towards community provision was also reflected in the 1962 White Paper, *Non-residential Treatment of Offenders Under 21*, which provided many pointers to the concept of intermediate treatment. Unlike the *Ingleby Report*, which reflected current child care practice that had developed beyond the scope of the 1948 Children Act, the 1962 White Paper turned to the United States for its inspiration. It used the experiences of the Boston Citizenship Training Group in formulating its proposals. It stressed peer-group work as an appropriate intervention with young offenders, and it noted the danger of 'contamination by association' if deviants were segregated into groups where criminal norms prevailed – as in residential establishments catering mainly for delinquents. This could be avoided if delinquents were treated in the community through facilities that were also available for non-delinquents, such as youth service and education provision.

The mid-sixties saw a further spate of political activity about juvenile crime, and much of it was sympathetic to the increasing involvement of social work in juvenile justice. Social workers had some powerful allies, especially within the intellectual élite of the Labour Party. The result, and the most tangible evidence of this support, was the publication of three documents – the Kilbrandon Committee report on *Children and Young Persons in Scotland* (April 1964), the Longford Committee report *Crime: a Challenge to Us All* (June 1964), and the White Paper *The Child, the Family, and the Young Offender* (August 1965).

The emphasis in these documents was on providing a family social work service as an antidote to delinquency. The recommendation was that family councils should replace juvenile courts. This was intended to reduce the stigma attached to court attendance and to allow more flexibility in meeting the changing needs of children and young people. These proposals were implemented in Scotland as part of the *Social Work (Scotland) Act*, 1968, where there was not the same inter-departmental squabbles, and inter-party conflicts, over these radical proposals as there was in England and Wales. In England and Wales responsibility for child care services and for penal policy lay with the Home Office, whereas other social work services were the responsibility of the recently created Department of Health and Social Security. There was also a much stronger Conservative Opposition in England and Wales. The result was three years of debate and consultation before a revised White Paper was published in 1968.

Children in Trouble reflected the influence of those pressure groups, such as the Magistrates Association, that had been campaigning for major amendments to the 1965 White Paper, but it also reflected the continuing emergence of social work as an increasing consideration in social policy and planning. The 1968 White Paper had obviously been influenced by those same social and criminological theories which were also influencing the young, newly (social science) trained personnel who were to be made responsible for the day-to-day enactment of its proposals. The White Paper stressed the normality of much delinquency and the fact that many young people who were delinquent were also deprived; indeed it assumed a causal link between deprivation and delinquency. The task, therefore, was to tackle this deprivation without stigmatizing the delinquent as deviant. Stigmatization, labelling, and the dangers of amplifying deviance by ostracizing a person from the community, were all dangers emphasized to the social worker-in-training by the 'new criminology'.

It was the 1968 White Paper that first described 'intermediate forms of treatment'. The intention was that the child should be treated as a member of his community, with others of his own age (not all of whom are delinquent), and although willing participation of the child in treatment was desirable, it was accepted that it might sometimes be necessary to have compulsory powers available – what Barbara Kahan called 'the iron fist in the velvet glove'. Hence the 1968 White Paper saw intermediate treatment as having a community and peer-group focus within the context of a family-orientated social work agency.

This family-orientated social work agency was the result of the deliberations of another committee. The Seebohm Committee had been convened in 1966 with a brief to 'review the organisation and responsibilities of the local authority personal social services and to consider what changes are desirable to secure an effective family service'. The work, and proposals, of this committee can also be related to the development of social policy for juvenile offenders:

> For those interested in achieving more fundamental changes than those just concerning delinquency, the issue of juvenile crime is useful as a springboard. By arguing that the prevention of juvenile delinquency is preferable to cure and that the former can only be achieved by a widespread improvement in social services, it is possible to construct a case for more general reforms. In the policy developments in both England and Wales, and Scotland, those interested in promoting a family service used the issue of juvenile delinquency to further their cause. (Hall, 1976)

That delinquency was a more burning political issue than welfare is well illustrated by the 'Crossman diaries' (Crossman, 1977). Crossman, as Secretary of State for Social Services, apparently showed little interest in the work of the Seebohm Committee; he was much more concerned about the conflicts within the National Health Service. Indeed, when the third reading of the Local Authorities Social Service Bill was taking place in Parliament Crossman had returned home to read in bed! By contrast, Callaghan, as Home Secretary, was much more centrally concerned with the Children and Young Persons Bill. After all, the tackling of crime was a major issue in the campaigns leading up to the General Election in June 1970 – an election the Labour Party was to lose only seven months after the passing of the Children and Young Persons Act, and only one month after the passing of the Local Authorities Social Services Act. The political and social tide had begun to turn. The waves of reaction and opposition to the reforms of the sixties continue to roll in the late 1970s. The ramifications of this defeat in 1970 of the Labour Government at that crucial stage of policy implementation (as compared to policy formulation) are still with us, as can be seen in relation to intermediate treatment.

The Legislative Model

It was the 1969 Act that provided a statutory framework for intermediate treatment. This legislative interpretation saw intermediate treatment as a sentencing option for magistrates and as a statutory responsibility of the newly emerging social services departments. This legislative model presented IT as:

(a) a sentence available to the courts following successful criminal or care proceedings for children or young persons up to age 17,

(b) a measure which could be added as an additional clause to a supervision order.

(c) This additional clause (section 12.2 (a) and/or (b)) gave discretion to the supervisor, as the representative of the Local Authority or the probation service, to require the supervisee to attend a facility of intermediate treatment,

(d) but this facility had to be of a type approved by the Secretary of State for Social Services, and had to be listed in the Regional Planning Committee's scheme for intermediate treatment.

(e) It was the responsibility of the Local Authority to make money available for intermediate treatment.

(Fig. 1.1 presents an algorithm of this statutory process.)

Fig. 1.1

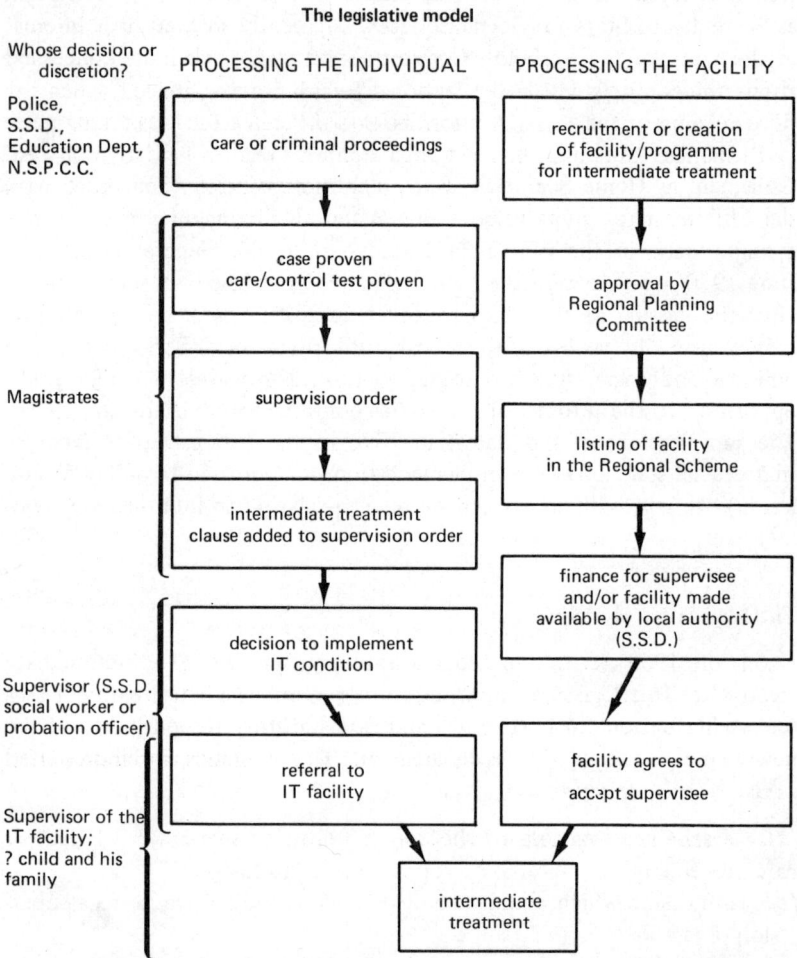

The legislative model

Whose decision or discretion?	PROCESSING THE INDIVIDUAL	PROCESSING THE FACILITY
Police, S.S.D., Education Dept, N.S.P.C.C.	care or criminal proceedings	recruitment or creation of facility/programme for intermediate treatment
Magistrates	case proven care/control test proven	approval by Regional Planning Committee
	supervision order	listing of facility in the Regional Scheme
	intermediate treatment clause added to supervision order	finance for supervisee and/or facility made available by local authority (S.S.D.)
Supervisor (S.S.D. social worker or probation officer)	decision to implement IT condition	
Supervisor of the IT facility; ? child and his family	referral to IT facility	facility agrees to accept supervisee
	intermediate treatment	

Some aspects of this legislative framework need stressing (and updating) as they are frequently misunderstood. First, an intermediate treatment clause can only be *added* to a supervision order following care or criminal proceedings for juveniles within the 1969 Act; intermediate treatment is *not* a sentence in its own right, as is, for instance, a community service order. Nor can it be added to a supervision order following matrimonial proceedings. Secondly, intermediate treatment, within the legislative framework, is not just about provision for adolescents. Any child or young person up to the age of 17 may have an IT clause added to a supervision order. Thirdly, the time dimensions for intermediate treatment in the 1969 Act have recently been amended. The Criminal Law Act, 1977, states that a child or young person can now be required to attend a facility of (intermediate) treatment for up to ninety days – no longer is there a distinction between the thirty- and ninety-day orders. The 1977 Act also allows that a supervised child who fails to comply with the requirements of a supervision order, including the IT conditions, made following criminal (*not* care) proceedings may be fined or required to attend an attendance centre, with the requirements of the original order still continuing.

Intermediate Treatment: An Identity Crisis

These amendments to the 1969 Act reflect a change in social attitudes and in political policy. Whereas with the 1969 legislation one could argue that its usefulness was largely in compelling *social workers* and their agencies to be more imaginative and constructive in working with young people in the community, the 1977 amendments emphasize coercion as a means of compelling the *young person* to involve himself in intermediate treatment. Indeed punishment is now propounded as a more likely solution to delinquency; treatment is seen as a soft option which has been found wanting. Throughout the 1970s this change has been gathering momentum, although it started initially with the return of the Conservative Government in 1970. Whole sections of the 1969 Act were never implemented. It was intended, for instance, that intermediate treatment would replace attendance centres and detention centres. However, rather than these centres being phased out, they are being used more and more. There are now a greater number of juveniles in penal confinement than at any time since 1908, and it is against this trend that intermediate treatment has had to fight for its survival. It has certainly had a deprived childhood and, now that it is 10 years old, it has to face an uncertain adolescence!

The return to deterrence and punishment, as opposed to prevention and treatment, is illustrated by the changing position of Sir Keith Joseph. It was Joseph who became Secretary of State for Social Services in the Conservative Government in 1970. In 1972 he wrote in support of intermediate treatment:

> The wider the opportunities and satisfactions which our society offers its members, the more acute are the problems of adjustment which it poses to a minority of young people. The factors which may lead to a child growing up feeling 'out of it all' are many. So are the ways in which the child's predicament can come to our notice – through truancy or non-achievement at school, through family

casework by one of the statutory or voluntary agencies for social service, or (all too often) through a first appearance before the courts. Plainly we need new ways in which we can help such young people to overcome their difficulties. (Department of Health and Social Security, 1972)

This is how Sir Keith welcomed intermediate treatment in 1972. In 1978, however, in a public lecture at the University of Bath, he painted a different picture:

More and more juvenile crime has been excused by a whole series of alibis. Either the bomb or the 'rotten system' or unemployment or poverty is used as an alibi or excuse . . . . I had come to the conclusion when in office, which is a conclusion from which I have not departed, that the social work world does not know how to help people to cope who cannot yet cope.

This disillusionment with social work as a means of tackling delinquency is also reflected in the debate in the House of Commons on the Report of the Expenditure Committee on the Children and Young Persons Act (Hansard, 1976). Social workers were criticized as being too young, too inexperienced, as not being concerned about the good of the community, and as being unskilled. The solutions offered to counter these perceived failings were to return powers of disposal to magistrates, to recruit older entrants to social work, and to make the probation service once again responsible for supervising juvenile offenders.

The Development of Intermediate Treatment

So far we have discussed two major features of intermediate treatment. First, intermediate treatment was, and is, a product of its time. It therefore reflects some of the confusions and conflicts to be found in social values and attitudes. Second, intermediate treatment was envisaged as a legislative, a social work, and a community response to delinquency and deprivation. It is apparent, therefore, that interpretations of IT's scope and potential have differed widely, and its development has varied depending on who has attempted to develop it, with what resources, and under the aegis of which agency. The differences in the development of intermediate treatment reflect the debate about its definition.

In the 1972 Department of Health and Social Security guide to intermediate treatment (for which Sir Keith Joseph had written the foreword) IT was defined as 'a flexible and discriminating use of the community's resources' (Department of Health and Social Security, 1972). The aim was to 'enrich [the child's] environment' and to 'assist his development'. This was to be achieved by bringing the child into contact with a new environment, to give him opportunities for forming new relationships, and to allow him to develop new interests. However, this booklet has subsequently been widely criticized (a little unfairly one might think) for encouraging a view of IT as sending kids in trouble to youth clubs ('table-tennis therapy') or up mountains on outward-bound courses ('sweating delinquency out through the pores of the skin'). Possibly these trends in the early days of intermediate treatment were as much a failure of the imagination of practitioners, their managers, and the Regional Planning Committees as of the Department of Health and Social Security.

Certainly at this time there was a great deal of confusion about what could be called intermediate treatment, and about who could receive it. Some social workers saw IT as a service to benefit all their young clients, others saw it as suitable for only a small minority. Some saw IT as primarily a social work service; others argued that it was more about social education and ought to be the responsibility of the youth service and the schools. Most agreed, however, that intermediate treatment was to be reserved largely for provision for adolescents. But was it just to be for adolescents who had been in trouble and who had appeared before the courts? Some local authorities reserved their intermediate treatment budgets for those who were the subject of IT orders. Others saw intermediate treatment as a means of considering and planning a community service for adolescents in general. If nothing else, intermediate treatment as an idea, and the responsibilities placed on local authorities by the 1969 Act to develop intermediate treatment, has achieved the not inconsiderable success of encouraging some (but not enough) social work agencies, and social work training courses, to look again at how a more effective community-based social work service can be provided for adolescents. It has also required that this service should attempt to consider, and to dovetail with, other community-based services and resources for young people. This is a theme that will be developed in this book, and which reflects our own thinking about intermediate treatment as 'an umbrella term for a wide range of both actual and potential community-based provision for adolescents (and children) who are deprived or who are more "at risk" of getting into trouble than their contemporaries'.

In practice, however, what happened initially is that social workers canvassed youth service facilities and voluntary youth organizations in an attempt to get them to take a quota of young people on intermediate treatment orders. It was these youth facilities which formed the bulk of the initial regional schemes for intermediate treatment. Difficulties arose when either the programmes available within these facilities were not seen as particularly appropriate to handle and work with the difficult behaviour of some of the adolescents, or else the supervising social worker saw himself as having a *personal* responsibility for developing his *own* relationship with the young person. Referral to another facility outside of the supervisory relationship might be an addition to supervision, but it often did little to make the supervisor–supervisee contact any more significant, influential, or relevant.

As a response to this perceived failure of IT, as a referral to a facility outside the supervisory relationship, to enrich the supervision offered to the adolescent, many social workers and probation officers initiated their own intermediate treatment programmes. In particular they turned to the model of activity groups as a favoured form of intermediate treatment. The knowledge that most young people who get into trouble do so in the company of their peers, and that the peer group is a particularly powerful influence during adolescence, provided an immediate cure for working with adolescents in trouble in the context of their peer group. These intermediate treatment groups had many diverse goals. We list below the goals of one actual group:

Aims of the Hay Lane IT Group

(a)   Increase the individual's sense of his own worth and capabilities.
(b)   Reduce his deviant status and likelihood of reoffending.
(c)   Provide an opportunity for open and trusting relationships with adults.
(d)   Break down cultural and environmental alienation.
(e)   Provide a base from which individual boys can progress either as individuals or groups into other organizations.
(f)   Enable the boys' families to cope better.
(g)   Provide a more effective means of statutory supervision.

Unfortunately all of these aims, it was unrealistically suggested, were to be achieved by map reading and compass exercises in the surrounding countryside once a week for a couple of hours, with two residential week-ends, over a period of a few months. It is not surprising that the validity and credibility of intermediate treatment began to be questioned, as is illustrated by this letter from a social work magazine:

> Without being too cynical, one can foresee a situation whereby IT can mean little more than a free holiday, with recipients advising their (social work) colleagues 'to get yourself on IT and you can have a free holiday with all expenses paid'. (Riley, 1974)

In some teams of social workers intermediate treatment still seems to have the status of a social worker's hobby, with residential periods seen as a holiday!

A response to the criticism that intermediate treatment activity groups are too short lived and that they are often not particularly relevant to the adolescent's everyday life (because they are usually composed of an 'artificial', social worker-selected peer group, rather than natural, neighbourhood-based friendship groups) has been to see intermediate treatment in a neighbourhood context (see Chapter 4). Working with volunteers recruited from the indigenous population, using neighbourhood facilities, locally-based community service projects, and detached youth work, all fit into this widening of the definition of intermediate treatment. At the same time as the definition of intermediate treatment has *broadened* there has also been a trend to *intensify* IT programmes. Intensive intermediate treatment attempts to offer a more influential package to the adolescent – a package that is more intensive in terms of time, impact, and effect. Day care, alternative schooling, and short-term, focused, residential care might all be included in an intensive intermediate treatment programme. These more intensive programmes have been facilitated by the emergence of IT centres.

Although the definition and practice of intermediate treatment may have broadened there is still an underlying philosophy of IT. Table 1.1 reflects some of the ways in which this philosophy may be applied. It also reflects the differing emphases possible within this philosophy. Intermediate treatment, however, continues to be concerned with adolescents in trouble; they may be delinquent and they may be deprived. The task for intermediate treatment is to reduce the various ways in which these young people are 'at risk': 'at risk' of continued offending, of continued deprivation, of reception into care, or of penal confinement. It attempts to counter deprivation, delinquency, and disturbance through programmes based on counselling and diversion. This may include elements of control, challenging the adolescent's picture of himself (and the picture others have of him) and offering an alternative self-concept, and also rehearsing new, less troublesome, but still rewarding, behaviours. Intermediate treatment also needs to be concerned with social policy, as well as social work practice. Influencing the workings of the juvenile justice system (see Table 1.1 and Chapter 6) and agency policies are also tasks for those involved in intermediate treatment.

Table 1.1 The range of intermediate treatment

ASSUMPTIONS	AIMS							
	INDIVIDUAL CHANGE → REDUCE DELINQUENCY ← SYSTEMS CHANGE					REDUCE DEPRIVATION		
	Break habit change values	Improve self-concept	Diversion	Maintenance	Radical reappraisal of the criminalization process	Emotional	Social	Material
Social learning model . . . delinquency is learnt behaviour	behaviour modifications show/rehearse alternative behaviours							
Negative self-concept leads to challenging and disruptive behaviour		experience success through legitimate activities – positive feedback from others						
Delinquency as opportunity and as a response to boredom			alternative activities and interests – integrate into youth provision					
Negative impact of labelling and institutionalization				monitoring and control in the community – may include day care, community service, etc.	decriminalization of status offences (e.g. truancy); increasing community tolerance – managing juvenile justice system			
Delinquents as victims: spontaneous remission of delinquent behaviour: normality of petty delinquency victims:								
Unsatisfactory relationships lead to disturbance, depression, and delinquency						developing trusting relationships with peers and caring adults		
Isolation and lack of social skills can lead to frustration, depression, and delinquency							integration into friendship group: social skills training	
Material deprivation stunts personal development								new horizons, new experiences, financial sponsorship

Why Intermediate Treatment?

So what theories underlie some of these forms and concerns of intermediate treatment? The theories discussed below are taken from the fields of criminology, social psychology, and social work:

(a) *Subcultural* theories of criminology see much delinquency as a response to social pressures. Delinquency is a reflection of how some people live within a culture that stresses fun, excitement, manliness, and rewards in the short term. This culture, in its turn, is a response to the inequalities of society, where the avenues to success are not equally open to everyone. Status frustration and blocked aspirations can all lead to the search for other means of achieving success and status. Delinquency might be one possible outcome. Intermediate treatment then comes into the picture as an attempt to control delinquency by offering other sources of fun, excitement, and desired status. Intermediate treatment might also include social skills training (like the skills involved in going for a job interview), or remedial education, which might increase the opportunities open to the individual. However, intermediate treatment in itself will not remove the basic inequalities in society, but it may go some way to influence social attitudes and, at a local level through a neighbourhood approach, it may be able to effect community tolerance of young people.

(b) Intermediate treatment can also be related to the view that delinquents *'drift'* in and out of delinquency. They are not full-time, committed delinquents, but they do sometimes commit (usually petty) offences in their search for fun and excitement. They are able to rationalize their law-breaking by 'techniques of neutralization' (Sykes and Matza, 1957). These techniques include:

Denial of responsibility . . . 'I didn't mean to do it.'
Denial of injury . . . 'well, no one got hurt.'
Denial of victim . . . 'it was a fair fight; they had it coming to them.'
Condemnation of the condemners . . . 'you're always picking on me; you're not fair.'
Appeal to higher loyalties . . . 'I only did it for my friends.'
These techniques of neutralization may be experienced by us as a process of castration: we feel impotent. Our young clients may not trust us, will not talk with us, and misinterpret our intentions. A part of our task, therefore, is to break down the barriers that exist between us and the adolescents, to neutralize these techniques of neutralization, to create situations where we can communicate with our young clients, and to increase our credibility with them. Intermediate treatment comes galloping over the horizon as an attempt at developing relationships of trust, respect,

understanding through the medium of shared activities. IT is aimed at aking down some of the barriers between worker and client.

(c) A further way in which intermediate treatment can be related to criminological theory, and this follows the idea of 'drifting' into delinquency, is that delinquent behaviour is not necessarily abnormal. However, by over-reacting to this behaviour we may actually confirm some adolescents in a delinquent identity. By labelling behaviour as deviant, and then ostracizing those who exhibit this behaviour from the community and from the company of non-delinquents (as in many community homes) can lead to *deviance amplification*, where further delinquency is encouraged. Intermediate treatment is an attempt to counter this process. IT is an alternative to residential care and penal confinement. It is an attempt to provide a more comprehensive service to kids living at home in their own neighbourhoods, and with their friends. It aims to challenge delinquent behaviour, but it also challenges the picture of the adolescent as just delinquent.

(d) Intermediate treatment can also be related to models from social psychology. The *deprivation* model suggests that some adolescents get into trouble because they are deprived of affection, acceptable models of responsible behaviour, and parental supervision, encouragement, and support. This model can be related to both sociology and social psychology, as deprivation may be social and material (low incomes, poor housing, bad schools) or emotional (little or inconsistent parental interest and love). Indeed these forms of deprivation are often linked; poor housing, poverty, and a decaying neighbourhood can lead to depressed, apathetic, and exhausted parents. Intermediate treatment is an attempt to counter some of these deprivations: by offering caring relationships, opportunities for holidays and hobbies, and some escape from the stresses and strains of home.

(e) But why all this emphasis on adolescents? One *model of adolescence* sees adolescence as a time of identity crisis, role experimentation, rule testing, and of fluctuating mood. Adolescence is also seen as a time of peer-group allegiance, with the peer group having a strong influence on the adolescent. Not the most promising of scenarios for the social worker with numerous young offenders on his caseload! Intermediate treatment comes to the rescue with its emphasis on working in the context of the peer group, of attempting to counter peer-group pressures towards delinquency, and by confronting and offering alternatives to difficult adolescent behaviour. IT should also be about looking at, and dealing with, some of the social and family attitudes that make adolescents angry and alienated.

(f) Lastly, intermediate treatment can also be related to social work philosophy and practice. By this we do not mean that because groupwork and community work are again fashionable, that this in itself is an adequate justification for intermediate treatment – after all, fashions, by definition, change. It is the *psychosocial emphasis of social work* which provides a rationale for intermediate treatment. This psychosocial emphasis should mean that as well as being concerned for and with the individual, we should care for him within his social surroundings. We should be concerned with the impact of his environment on him, and of his impact on the environment. If this is so then we should be involved with the client in his environment – with his family, his friends, his school, his neighbourhood.

The suggestion throughout this chapter (and throughout this book) is that the scope of intermediate treatment is wide, and the tasks that have been set for it are strenuous. We return to issues about the general development (or underdevelopment) of intermediate treatment towards the end of this book (Chapter 6), but we now turn to some suggestions about the actual practice of some of the techniques which may be used by those involved in intermediate treatment. We start by looking at the formation of groups because, as suggested above, groupwork has become popularly associated with intermediate treatment.

2. A Framework for Planning Groups

Two common mythologies seem to have arisen in recent years, aided by reflective articles and accounts of practice: first, that intermediate treatment and groupwork are interchangeable terms, particularly in the context of social services departments, and secondly, that groupwork in intermediate treatment automatically means 'activity' groups. In this chapter it is our intention to examine the basis for groupwork in IT, and also to offer a framework by which workers can both consider and plan their groupwork intervention more effectively. In doing this we will hopefully explore the two statements outlined above.

Considering Groupwork

Perhaps the most important decision taken when planning to run a group is the decision not to do so. While such a statement might well sound like a quote from *Alice in Wonderland*, there are some strong arguments for making it. In the first instance it is sometimes better for the idea of running groups to be used not as an end in itself, but as a 'thought process breaker'.

It has often been argued that social work agencies offer a service only on an individual basis, regardless of whether or not it is an appropriate response to the problem being presented. This difficulty of breaking away from the traditional way of looking at things is not an unusual one. However, if people can be freed from looking only for established responses, for instance by considering to run a group, the potential for discovering different methods of solving or working with a problem becomes a greater possibility. In an atmosphere that is both acceptable and encouraging to the discovery of new ideas, many different options may well be generated. In the end perhaps neither groupwork nor casework is used, but a new approach or combination of approaches may evolve.

This appeal for us to be flexible in our thinking rather than rigid, has much in common with the work of Edward de Bono and lateral thinking; in Chapter 6 there will be further discussion of how alternative thinking strategies might be used to aid the development of intermediate treatment. For the present it is sufficient to say that groupwork has both the potential to be as established and conservative as any other social work response, or it can act as a stimulus for a wide variety of alternatives.

The second stage in considering groupwork comes when the worker wishes to translate his ideas into reality. Many people have spoken and written of the difficulties they have encountered when setting up particular schemes. These difficulties often relate to either one or a combination of the following: poor management or supervision, lack of skills and training, limitations of the resources available, or poor preparation and planning. While this chapter has been conceived with the last category in mind, offering both a framework and a discussion for preparing groupwork projects, hopefully it also has an impact on the other three categories. Good preparation is likely to stimulate support from your management system, or at least give you a better basis for arguing your case for both resources and support.

Before we consider further the effects of using groupwork as an appropriate response to intermediate treatment, three provisos should be added:

(a)   The only valid reason for starting a group is that it is the *best* possible means available *at that time* for solving or coping with a need that has been discovered or expressed.

(b)   No matter how good an idea is, or how much personal investment has been placed in that idea, it might always be capable of improvement or of being substituted for a better scheme.

(c)   The development of intermediate treatment, as yet another vested and segregated interest area, would seem to us to be both counter-productive to the needs of social work, and to the section of society it seeks to help.

Our intention is, therefore, to argue that intermediate treatment is an umbrella concept for an area of work that involves a wide variety of techniques, methods, and intensities of involvement in which groupwork is only one, albeit significant, part.

Forming and Preparing Groups

Clearly in groupwork there are important distinctions to be made between groups that are formed by the worker, and existing groups which ask for or receive a worker's services. In this section of the book we are mainly concerned with the groups that are formed by workers, although there are often occasions when the two areas overlap, just as there are many principles of group dynamics which are relevant to both streams of work. It would therefore be dangerous to ignore in a formed group the possible peer-group relationships that might already be in existence, just as it would be dangerous to assume that natural groups do not have defined stages to their lives and, for instance, issues and concerns over authority and leadership.

Having established that using groupwork could be one of several possibilities available, what are the reasons that make it advantageous as compared to other methods? Tom Douglas (1976) advances the following:

(a)   That there is already a group problem.
(b)   To use peer learning, e.g. Alcoholics Anonymous.
(c)   To make beneficial use of group pressures.
(d)   To make beneficial use of group interaction.
(e)   To make beneficial use of group support systems.
(f)   To make beneficial use of the social nature of group meetings.
(g)   To make beneficial use of the resources of the group.

There are, however, almost as many reasons for not forming a group, such as:

(a)   'Wouldn't it be a good idea if we were to put all these people into a group'. The underlying aim might only be to facilitate the task of the worker by seeing several people at once, and not that grouping those people together would provide the best approach to their problems. We could call this 'the economy response'.

(b)   'Other parts of our department/division/county/organization have run groups, it's about time we did' — the competitive response.

(c)   'We've got some workers who want or need to run groups, so we can look around and find clients that need it' — 'the worker satisfaction'/ 'social work student response'.

(d)   'We've tried everything else, so we might as well run a group' — 'the despair response'.

The key to effective preparation lies in questioning; questioning yourself, your motivation, your agency, your colleagues, until in the end all people party to the formation of a group are clear about what is intended. This is especially important if you feel that you might be faced with the task of 'selling' what you have to offer to a relatively disbelieving client, colleague, or management. There is also an obvious relationship between clarity of intent, security, and commitment. If you are unsure about what you are going to do or why, then it is not going to be easy for others to feel committed to it. In such a situation it is not hard to see why some workers offer 'hypothetical goodies' or promises which are impossible to fulfil in an attempt to gain either the co-operation of their agency or the attendance of group members.

Sometimes another problem is getting people to explain what exactly it is that they intend to do. This defence is most often given voice in the lines: 'I'm only going to run a simple play/activity/discussion session, I can't be bothered/haven't got the time, to go through a whole load of preparation.' However, even the simplest of schemes can often develop problems which are common to many groups, and this is often the result of inadequate preparation. Perhaps the following sentence should be cut out and pinned up in any department likely to run a group:

MORE GROUPS PROBABLY RUN INTO DIFFICULTIES,
END PREMATURELY, OR ELSE FAIL TO ACHIEVE THEIR
POTENTIAL GOALS, THROUGH INADEQUATE PREPARATION
THAN FOR ANY OTHER REASON.

The checklist printed below is intended to help overcome some of the problems and, together with the subsequent discussion, improve the quality of preparation for groups. It can help you to examine what your potential group is actually about, and also to identify some of the 'hazy' danger areas that commonly arise once the group has been formed (see also Hodge, 1977; Personal Social Services Council, 1977; Social Work Service Development Group, 1977).

There are two methods of answering the questions we pose. Obviously you can start at the beginning of Section 1 and work through to the end of Section 4. However, some people have found this difficult because it can mean answering the hardest questions first. Therefore you can go through and answer, or attempt to answer, the questions that you find easiest, and then go back and answer those that you have missed out. In using this second method it is vitally important that the answers you initially give do not then contradict the answers you write later. Some workers have also found it helpful when answering to have an independent *'agent provocateur'*/consultant asking the questions and testing out the 'honesty' or 'realism' of the answers. If the exercise proves impossible, then it is a good indication that something could be wrong. Perhaps another method of work is more appropriate, or not enough time has been allowed to prepare appropriately. Whatever the reason, it is better to sort the problem out now before the group actually starts.

The Checklist*

Section 1: Group Purpose and Method

1. What is the main purpose of the group? . . . .

. . . .

. . . .

2. Are there any secondary purposes? . . . .

. . . .

. . . .

. . . .

. . . .

. . . .

. . . .

3. What type of group is it, e.g. *(a)* leisure activity, *(b)* educational, *(c)* social treatment, *(d)* mixed, *(e)* other? . . . .

4. Method, e.g. *(a)* play, *(b)* drama and role play, *(c)* talk, *(d)* movement, *(e)* work, *(f)* total community, *(g)* mixed? . . . .

5. What kind of theoretical base is to be used? . . . .

. . . .

. . . .

. . . .

*Many of the basic questions, although not the format, are derived from Douglas (1976).

6. By what title is the group to be known? . . . .

. . . .

Section 2: Selection

7. How will members be selected:

   (a) On what basis? . . . .

   (b) Functioning age range? . . . .

   (c) Sex distribution? . . . .

   (d) How many? . . . .

   (e) From where will they come? (e.g. social background, can other

      agencies refer to the group?) . . . .

   (f) Intelligence? . . . .

   (g) Ability to verbalize? . . . . (if necessary)

   (h) Who does the selecting? . . . .

   (i) Any other relevant factors? . . . .

Section 3: Group Operation, Leadership, and Recording

8. Where will the group meet? . . . .

9. How long will each session last? . . . .

10. How frequently will the group meet? . . . .

11. For how long? . . . .

12. At what time? . . . .

13. How many group leaders will be needed; what roles will they play?

   . . . . (name who they are)

   . . . .

14. What style of leadership is involved (e.g. permissive, directive, etc.)?

....

....

....

15. Will the sessions be recorded? What method will be used? ....

....

....

Section 4: Important Factors External to the Group

16. Does the proposed group fit into the department's policy? ....

....

17. Is it possible with the resources available, if not, what is needed

    and can it be obtained? ....

....

....

....

....

18. Is transport available (if necessary)? ....

....

19. Have you explained to your colleagues what you are trying to do?

....

20. Will individual social work sessions be available for members, in
    addition to the group, *(a)* with whom, *(b)* when?

....

....

....

21. What facilities for consultation can you use/should be obtained?

How frequently will you and the consultant meet? . . . .

. . . .

. . . .

. . . .

Section 1: Group Purpose and Method

The primary question to be answered (*'What is the real purpose of this group?'*) is often the most difficult question. Ideally it should be possible to encompass a purpose or objective in one or two sentences, simple enough in construction and wording to make sense to whoever needs to know, be they client, colleague, or yourself. The three most frequent pitfalls are making the statement very generalized and full of cliches; so complicated that it does not really make sense to anyone; or producing two explanations which then make it difficult if you are trying to get both group members and leaders to work towards a common goal. For example:

'This group offers a therapeutic and educational interaction between social work supervisor and child.' If this is intended as the main purpose (as it was when first written) for a group of 10- to 12-year-olds, then:

(a) it is a vague concept for the workers to implement,
(b) the kids are not going to understand it; and
(c) even if they could understand it, they probably would not agree that they needed it, and are much more likely to view the group as a 'bit of a laugh' or a chance to have fun.

Although 'having a bit of fun' might well be a legitimate purpose, if the workers at some point in the group's life wish to look at mutual problems and difficulties that the members have, then the discussion can easily be avoided by the members saying that it is not really what the group is about. While not wishing to suggest hypothetical purposes that could detract from the need to make statements relevant to any one particular group, some of the suggestions in Table 2.1 offer simple statements of the possible purpose and aims of IT groups.

When we are defining objectives it is necessary to make sure that the group represents a response to a real need being expressed, and, as mentioned before, that it is the best means available of achieving its resolution. Because time equals investment (both financial and emotional) there is often an understandable reluctance to abandon the idea of forming

Table 2.1 *Some models of IT groups*

Need to be fulfilled	Aims of work	Main content of group programme	Possible evaluation methods to be used	Additional comments
A variety of bored kids who lack adequate supervision and stimulation over school holidays.	To provide fun and occupation of time. (Group has a strong 'here and now' emphasis.)	Structured activities based on fun and enjoyment.	Simple questions, e.g. Did people attend? Did they enjoy themselves?	Like holiday play-scheme; often used for children of single parent families.
Desire to develop a particular hobby or skill based on existing interest.	Hobby and/or skill development. (Here, now, and *afterwards* orientation.)	Task-centred activities; often links with other established groups depending on skill sought, e.g. judo, fishing club.	Measurement of degree of skill attained (e.g. number of fish caught, ability to cast, etc.). Is hobby continued at end of the group?	Need not necessarily be pursued as a group. Requires expertise.
Need to develop social skills for improved existence, e.g. performance and presentation at job interview.	To improve basic social skills.	Following structured tasks, using basic techniques such as role play, etc.	Self- and group-evaluation questionnaires.	Group uses a wide variety of techniques to achieve fairly straightforward objectives.
An improvement in poor relationships with adults and/or peers.	To build relationships between social worker and adolescent, or adolescent and adolescent.	Uses various activities and exercises that facilitate communication and relationship building.	Sociograms, interaction scales.	Most frequently (and often over-)used rationale for groupwork in IT.
Avoidance of major crisis, e.g. reception into care, family breakdown, Borstal training, etc.	Increase in personal awareness, to rehearse alternatives to/and consequences of particular actions. To utilize adolescents' ability to avert crisis.	Characterized by intensity, closeness of members to members, and members to leaders; varied tasks; similar to therapeutic community model.	Process records. Vignette responses. Evaluation by significant others. Self-concept evaluation. Whether pending crisis is averted.	Kind of group that often takes different forms. Mainly characterized by intensity of involvement, both in terms of time and staff/member ratio.

a group once the process of formation has been initiated. Groups often start even when it is apparent to everyone that they have been formed for the wrong reasons, or with an unachievable goal. To start such a group is dangerous, for who you select, style of leadership, and how you record, should be intrinsically bound to the purpose of the group.

Having argued that it is important not to have two explanations for the group, Question 2 on the checklist might seem contradictory. Here we are not talking about the central theme of the group, but about secondary objectives which can be classified as the possible 'spin-off' benefits of the group. The reason for attempting to identify these at the start rather than at the end of the group's life, is basically to provide an aid to recognizing trends and movements during the group's operation. For example, a situation can arise where the group members and the leaders are ostensibly working together on the main purpose of the group, while everyone covertly knows and accepts that they are really tackling another problem. Reading descriptions of intermediate treatment projects quickly indicates how frequently this can occur.

We mentioned in Chapter 1 (p. 10) the kind of group which has a plethora of goals, some so ambitious as to do justice to the entirety of social work, or a government manifesto, but which aims to achieve them by a mixture of mountain climbing and table tennis. This is not to condemn the use of activities and games in groups, but to try and put them into some sort of perspective. The framework should therefore be one where the activities are a means to an end – such as to stimulate discussion, reduce isolation, or to improve self-esteem. Hopefully they are also only one of several methods used to reach that objective. The group which has such an extensive programme of activities that it neither leaves the time, nor the breath, for discussion can scarcely be maximizing its potential for help.

A variety of things can therefore be said about the purpose of a group:

(a) It should be straightforward, and comprehensible to whoever needs to understand its aims.

(b) It should be something achievable by the members of the group.

(c) It should be possible to measure whether or not you have achieved your objective.

(d) It should be meeting an identified need.

Table 2.1 offers five possible models, based on groups with which the authors have worked in the past. What it does not represent is a blueprint on which to model groups, because different or alternative needs and aims will result in different programmes and evaluations.

Fig. 2.1

Crucial interacting variables on selection

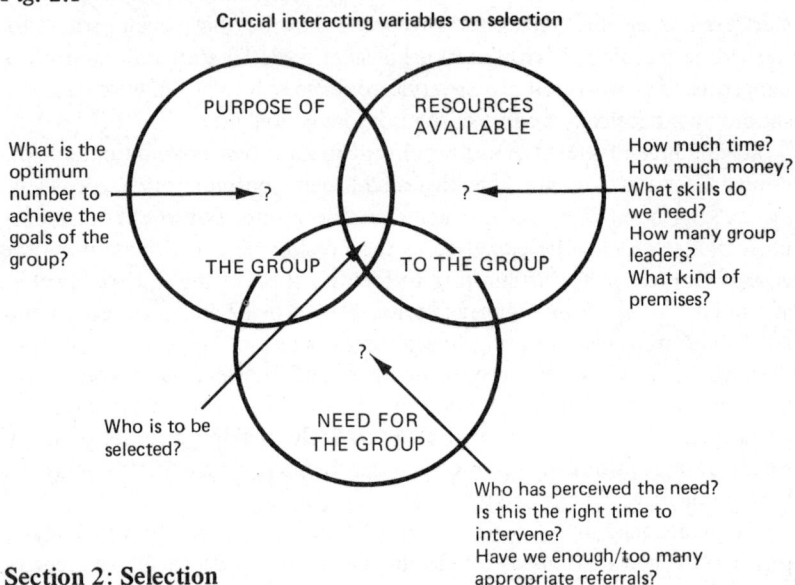

What is the
optimum
number to
achieve the
goals of the
group?

PURPOSE OF

RESOURCES
AVAILABLE

?

?

THE GROUP

TO THE GROUP

How much time?
How much money?
What skills do
we need?
How many group
leaders?
What kind of
premises?

?

Who is to be
selected?

NEED FOR
THE GROUP

Who has perceived the need?
Is this the right time to
intervene?
Have we enough/too many
appropriate referrals?

Section 2: Selection

The problem of allocating time and social work resources can cause
serious problems in the selection of group participants. Often where no
particular post is designed for intermediate treatment it is only those
social workers who have a caseload weighted towards adolescents, or
else who make their own leisure time available, who can become involved
in working with groups. In the case of the former, an additional problem
can sometimes occur, i.e. time can only be allocated if a preponderance of
those workers' clients are included in the group. This in turn pre-empts
any selection procedures, which can mean that the membership of a group
is decided even before its purpose is agreed, or else one goes through the
motions of a mock selection when a part of the composition of the group
has been predetermined. Such difficulties over selection can then be
further compounded if it is the first group that the agency has operated,
or if it is the only group functioning at one particular time in this client
area. It has not been uncommon for children's ages to be 'altered', or for
their particular problem to be exaggerated or minimized, so that they
then 'fit' the criteria for selection set by the groupworkers. While such
practices are understandable in terms of the limited opportunities for
participation in any group, it can obviously have serious consequences
when, for example, you find that you have an age differential of five
years instead of two. This is in addition to other problems that may
occur, such as the social worker simply having no idea that 'calm, slightly

withdrawn, Harry' in the office interview setting is in fact the local gang leader, and a real tearaway by anybody's description – particularly his own. The lack of accurate information prior to running a group is a constant complaint of the groupworkers that we meet.

Two further key issues also occur with unfailing regularity when discussing problems of selection: first, what is the right number, and, secondly, should they all have the same problem? The answer to the first question is fairly simple, i.e. there is no such thing as the right number; what is right for one group can be totally wrong for another. If you want to run a summer holiday playscheme, three members would be too small; conversely, a discussion group looking at personal traumas and worries would be rather tricky with a membership of thirty. The size of the group, as Fig. 2.1 suggests, should be decided when considering a combination of interacting variables.

Fig. 2.1 represents some of the factors likely to be involved in selecting members for a group. Examining the interaction of the three areas in the figure should give an indication of the appropriate number to be selected. For example, if the need is for a project for adolescents who are close to being received into residential care then it might call for special skills, a high level of adult/adolescent interaction, and a large sum of money. This in turn could determine that it should only be available for a small number of people if it is to achieve its purpose. The converse might well be true of a mainly activity-orientated group, where the goal is to provide alternative interests for the adolescents in order to divert them from continuing delinquency.

The following points about size should be borne in mind; the larger a group is then:

(a) the less time becomes available for each individual person to contribute,

(b) some activities can still only be performed on an individual or small group basis, or are much better when done that way (e.g. special reading tuition),

(c) the more any one activity might cost (e.g. going swimming),

(d) the less equipment becomes available for each person, or much more has to be purchased,

(e) if the group is going to have a period in residence, it might be harder to find accommodation,

(f) the number of ideas elicited from group members increases or their range is wider, and it becomes more difficult to reach agreement,

(g) the group has more opportunity for dividing into factions, and less need to tolerate minorities.

In looking at the issue of whether one should select individuals who are similar or dissimilar, there are some additional factors to be considered. Clearly there are several advantages to groups where the members have shared problems; the opportunity to have the same personal goal for everyone, and to discuss shared concerns and anxieties, becomes available.

However, where difficulties, defences, and methods of coping with problems are shared, there is the possibility that the problem-identity of the group is reinforced and the 'false view of reality' (e.g. 'Everyone who comes *into care* nicks from each other, just look round this group') acts as a collusive force against whatever 'reality' the worker is trying to present.

Other 'similarity' issues include the balance of age and sex. For example, a mature 13-year-old girl, although perhaps having a need to act in an immature way on occasions, is more likely to feel comfortable with a 15-year-old of the same sex, than an immature boy of her own age. Having one girl in a group of eight boys, or vice versa, is a situation also likely to lead to difficulties. Mixing degrees of problem or disadvantage can create varying intensities of involvement for different people in the group. Creating groups where either individual goals are set for each member, or else widely different problems tackled, can mean jealousy, isolation, and lack of cohesion, unless tackled with a high staff/adolescent ratio and a good deal of involvement.

However, differing behaviours can be drawn to the group's attention and used as a cue to focus on the group's performance and to get individuals to look at their own behaviour. Bullying, scapegoating, being disruptive, and individual isolation and withdrawal, are issues that the group can usefully discuss.

Finally, if you have not been completely put off the whole idea of selection and opted to work with self-selecting groups instead, there is the troublesome problem of who actually selects? Hopefully this would be, or at least include, the people or person who is going to run the group. In many agencies, though, there are other considerations to take into account. For instance, is it necessary to include your:

(a)   supervisor(s) or line manager(s) in the discussions?
(b)   Should your consultant be involved?
(c)   What explanations should be given about those referrals not accepted?
(d)   Will your decisions be readily accepted?

Unless the process of selection is clear, precise, and agreed then comments such as the following can easily arise: 'I thought [did he/she?] that you had offered him a place in the group, rather than just considering him, and now he's so excited I can't possibly tell him that he hasn't been selected', or 'I know little Freddy doesn't *quite* fit the purpose of your group [note that he probably does not fit it at all, and it has also now become 'your group' rather than 'ours'], but couldn't you fit him in somehow because there won't be another group like this for months.'

Section 3: (Questions 8 to 12)

Group Operation

Questions 8 to 12 on the checklist are concerned with essential and obvious practicalities about the operation of the group. The most frequent challenge to answering these questions is clearly 'If the group is going well, then why shouldn't we extend its life or length?'. Partly this depends on the initial definition of purpose. Even if the group is fairly open-ended, as might be expected for instance with a 'drop-in' centre for adolescents, then hours of opening, and the total length of time for which the service will be available, are obviously significant if people are to feel secure in using such a facility. Making a commitment (whether offering or receiving a service) requires some information about the amount of time available, whether we are talking about a meeting, an interview, or a group session.

It is also necessary to examine realistically whether time and availability are appropriate to the purpose you are attempting to achieve. For example, if the service is for adolescents in some kind of crisis, then is being available once a fortnight frequent enough for the degree of impact and accessibility necessary to relieve that crisis? In groups that have a firm structure the issue of ending can still be disputed by statements such as 'We can set it up for three months and then review its continuation.' This can only be acceptable if that is what is genuinely intended; when, for example, some of the group leaders are leaving at that point, or there is uncertainty over whether further funding will be available. In *most* situations it is preferable to determine a set finishing point, so that the group can end on a high note, rather than just dwindling away.

The fundamental issue behind these questions is basically one of security. Knowing how long the group will run, where, and when, enables both workers and members alike to know what commitment is being asked of them. Many of the adolescents in IT groups lead such uncertain lives anyway that to add to that uncertainty by our own intervention would be morally wrong. Having a definite structure also aids the leaders in the planning and programming of a group. A further point is that if the length of sessions varies, this can then lay the whole group open to manipulation, such as holding tempting insights or problems back to the end of a group session as a means of prolonging its duration.

In a group where the mode of contact changes, for example from an evening meeting to a residential week-end, then further implications for planning are involved. A general maxim is that the more group interaction is compressed, for instance from two hours a week to a twenty-four-hour block period, so the pace at which the group passes through the stages of group development is also accelerated. One worker's report illustrates this quite well:

> When we came to our long residential week-end at the end of the group, we [the group leaders] were apprehensive over how well this might work. To our surprise it was a very successful event. Where the group had previously been marred by challenges to our changing leadership and splitting-off into various cliques, it now became cohesive and there was a feeling of closeness that we had never achieved before. Our only regret was that we made this progress just as the group was finishing, and we all wished that we had gone away together earlier in the group.

Another issue for many IT groups is where to meet. Several survive quite successfully with venues apparently inadequate for the group's purpose (one of the authors ran a daily project for three months from a garden shed!). However, it is important, or at least it makes the leaders' task easier, if premises are suitable. Where you use a building that is shared with other sections of the community, then this means covering issues in your preparation such as which rooms/equipment can be used, who pays for breakages, and is it possible to monitor all the available space? Even a small matter such as confirming dates can become an issue, as one group discovered on arriving to use the local community centre when they were suddenly confronted by an O.A.P.'s bingo session reaching a heady, and not to be interrupted, climax. Another worker found that even using premises belonging to his own agency was not an ideal solution. If you meet in rooms attached to office accommodation then there is a danger of confidential files, memos, and reports being seen by the adolescents as they dash to the toilet for a subterranean smoke, and stop off on the way to scribble impolite graffiti on notice-boards and desk-top blotters.

Section 3: (Questions 13 and 14)

Leadership

Tom Douglas (1976) writes that 'most group workers when starting with a group are concerned not so much with the theoretical aspects of leadership, but with the practical problems of exercising such a role and being able to assess how their leadership efforts can be made more effective'. Both research and practice records demonstrate that groups both expect and demand leadership from a groupworker and that anxieties arise when that role is not accepted (Jones, 1979).

Clearly there are differences in both role expectations and performance when a leader is working with a natural formation, such as a family or an existing friendship group of peers, as compared to a group that he has structured and selected. The very process of selection puts the leader into a 'key-person' role, for he is responsible for people being present, and for convening the group. This is one factor that helps to make the purpose of the group far more that of the leaders than that of the members. Table 2.2 represents four leadership styles that are often found in intermediate treatment groups and it highlights some of their associated advantages and disadvantages.

Table 2.2 Four leadership styles

Leadership styles	Characteristic advantages	Characteristic disadvantages
Authoritarian/ responsible	Group has sense of direction or of goals to be achieved. Develops feelings of security. Helps to produce cohesion among group members. Can help other leaders to play complementary roles. Works best with younger group members.	Allows little chance for group to decide to change direction. Often results in some of the other leaders or group members leaving the group. Allows few opportunities for group members to take responsibility.
Laissez-faire	Invests much more power in the group. Allows for democratic decision-making. Lets group programme be flexible to need. Works best with older group members.	Often covers a lack of knowledge/information of what the group is really about. Leaders rarely seem to know what each other is doing. Can be interpreted as weakness on the part of leaders. Group aimlessly wanders from one point to another trying to decide what it is doing without adequate points of reference.

Leadership styles	Characteristic advantages	Characteristic disadvantages
Task-orientated	Tasks in the group can be divided between leaders, e.g. 1. responsible for obtaining resources and services 2. responsible for liaison with other agency staff and recording 3. responsible for activities in the group. Allows leaders to concentrate on areas at which they are most proficient.	Can produce confusion over who is actually doing what. Sometimes difficult to define boundaries between different tasks. Sufficient time has to be allowed for adequate communication to take place between group leaders. Many group issues will span many task areas.
Combination	Combines all or some of the above methods, allowing for a flexible response which is appropriate to the needs demonstrated by the group.	Makes members unsure of where they stand in relation to the leaders. Often personified by one leader who is *'laissez-faire'* for 90 per cent of the group and who then becomes extremely authoritarian when some major/minor crisis occurs.

A primary characteristic of the group leader's role is the need to be consistent and reliable. Three factors often seem to occur in IT groups which can lead to failure to meet this need:

(a) If you are planning a long-term group, recognize constraints that can affect it. For example, many social services departments until very recently have had a high turnover of staff. Hence, if a group was planned to last for one or two years, it would be very likely to end with completely different leaders from those with which it started. It might end prematurely and unplanned if the staff leave and there is no one to carry it on.

(b) Try and avoid a changing or 'rotating' staff system, or even a succession of visitors in a newly established group. If this does occur then group members often respond by confusion over who is supposed to be there, longer time will be spent in conflict with the leaders, and it can involve members opting out of the group altogether.

(c) Consistency between leaders is also at its most tenuous when groups are newly formed, when co-leaders have never worked together before, or when differences between leaders have not been adequately resolved.

The failure to resolve differences or problems is illustrated by the following quote from the report of a probation officer who ran, with two of his colleagues, a group based on improving social skills and peer-group relationships for certain probationers:

> The question arose at the end of our session as to whether the workers would meet some of the members of our group and go to the pub. The worker who was asked didn't answer the question at this point as the group was just finishing, but said that he would talk to the others in their consultation session (this immediately followed the group). In the session the worker left it until the end to raise this matter, and although we had a hurried discussion no decision was reached. This was partly because we thought the lads would have gone off anyway, rather than hang around. This indecision was quickly exposed when on stepping outside the building two of the group members popped up from behind a car and said 'Are you coming to the pub?' One of us replied 'yes', another 'no', and the third didn't answer. After a variety of exchanges, the two members were eventually invited, but then proceeded to say that they didn't want to come because of the disagreements. Although the issue was discussed and resolved in later groups, it was something that the two members frequently referred to, and partly succeeded in using as a manipulative tool over ourselves, especially as we recognized it as a moment of weakness.

Being insistent when planning a group that a decision is reached, mutually agreed, and that it is able to be carried out should be seen as a sign of strength, rather than pettiness.

In discussing the number of leaders that will be required to operate the group, again it seems better to talk in terms of various interacting factors rather than stating any particular right or wrong number. The following points all relate to the number of leaders which might be appropriate:

(a)   The more leaders there are, then the greater the amount of time that can be devoted to any one individual group member.

(b)   There are, however, obvious limitations to this, as when the number of leaders becomes such as either to intimidate group members or even out number them.

(c)   Workers who are inexperienced or lacking in confidence often prefer a group that has several other leaders. This can sometimes confirm insecurity by confirming that person in an 'observer' or 'assistant' role, rather than helping him to acquire or try out new skills. There is a much greater possibility for confusion, rather than safety, in numbers.

(d)   Monitoring and supervising throughout the premises where the group operates can become a problem. It is, therefore, important to have a leadership/group member ratio capable of working within the premises available; for example, thirty adolescents, two leaders and six rooms is a bad formula, because:

(i)   you will not be able to remain in contact with the total group at any one time, and
(ii)   it becomes easy for control and containment to supersede any other purpose that the group might be attempting to achieve.

(e)   The trend in leadership is to have at least one male and one female worker in most IT groups. While not essential, it is often appropriate to avoid combinations such as an all-male leadership of a group of female adolescents.

(f)   Finally, there are certain statements that can indicate potential leadership problems, such as:

(i)   'I might be a bit late for the first few weeks' (often means 'I probably won't come at all');

(ii)   'I really feel that the female workers should do the shopping/washing-up' (rarely stated quite as explicitly, but often covertly intended);

(iii)   'I think it will be quite safe for us to go to the pub for an evening when we take the group camping'. (Taking groups into residence, we feel, implies responsibility which does not mean that the day finishes at 5.30 p.m., or when the group members have gone to sleep. Two group reports presented to the authors have talked of major crises when the group leaders have vanished for a drink in the evening. One was caused by the group leaders getting drunk themselves, and the second by splits between the leaders over who, if anybody, was going to remain in charge.)

Section 3: (Question 15)

Recording

The final issue in this section on group operation is about *recording*, a subject frequently ignored. There is a considerable feeling in social work that recording is an irrelevance, or at least a handicap, rather than an aid to the work being undertaken. Many group records in intermediate treatment are closer to anecdotal accounts than to records which can help improve performance and allow for evaluation.

We feel that recording should attempt to satisfy the following conditions:

(a)   It should be easy and simple to complete (a rough formula could be five minutes for each hour of group contact).

(b)   It should be orientated to the purpose of the group. For example, while some factors related to group dynamics (such as relationship patterns) should be monitored, the importance given to these and the inclusion of other areas, such as the degree of group cohesion, or the ability of the

group to concentrate on and achieve particular goals, will vary according to the stated purpose of the group.

(c) The recording should assist group leaders to gain understanding of trends and movements within the group.

(d) Where appropriate, group members should be involved in recording, and certainly in evaluating.

(e) From the records made it should be possible to start to evaluate the success or failure (or aspects of both) of the group.

Section 4: Important Factors External to the Group (Questions 16 to 21)

This last section of the checklist, although not central to the group's operation, can still have a major effect on its planning and eventual outcome. The questions here can be related to the final chapter on 'The Politics of Intermediate Treatment'.

The most frequently offered answer to the question 'Does the proposed group fit departmental policy?' is that 'Our department doesn't have a policy!' Many groups give the appearance of occurring *despite* the agency from which they stem, rather than because of it. Such a situation arises because groups are often run in the worker's own time, on shoe-string budgets, and for social workers they are seen as an optional extra to 'getting on with your caseload'. They are rarely effectively researched or even used as a consistent option for consideration in case reviews. While much can be laid at the door of a management system that has allowed this to happen, often workers also have covertly accepted or even agreed with this approach, appreciating the freedom that it has allowed for their individual style of work.

If groupwork within intermediate treatment is to flourish then it needs to achieve a much more professional basis than at present. The provision of groups based on established needs, and appropriate responses, should have a planned development within a department's policy. If it is based on a perceived need with real opportunities for a flexible response, then the groups proposed for the future should be far more varied than at present. It is not uncommon for the once-a-week activity group to be seen as a response to all ills, ranging from social isolation to the avoidance of residential care. It is therefore as much a responsibility of the individual worker(s) to encourage discussion of their group proposals, to seek appropriate supervision, and to ask for recompense for the work undertaken, as it is for management to provide it. It is not hard to see that real progress has taken place only in those agencies that have developed a coherent policy towards intermediate treatment, involving both workers and management.

Question 17 relates to the need to make adequate plans and provision before the group actually starts. Questions such as 'Are there sufficient funds in the IT budget to pay for the two residential weeks we have planned?' should be tackled before promises or commitments about such events are made to the group.

Working out in advance from where resources are coming, and who is going to obtain them, is vital if the amount of time that can be devoted to running the group is limited.

Informing colleagues about your intention is both a form of insurance and support, and essential where the group is only one part of a wider form of assistance that might be offered to any particular individual, family, or community. This involves making sure if you are asking for referrals to a potential group, that everyone knows when and what kind of information you require. It means exchanging reports on individual progress inside and outside the group with those workers who made the referrals, and agreeing a framework between groupworker and case-worker for reaching decisions about a client. In some social work teams the responsibility for arranging 'cover' when away from the office can also devolve on to the individual, who then has to seek the support and co-operation of his colleagues. Hopefully, if the agency already has established policies and procedures, some framework for most of these points will already be in existence.

To tackle the issues mentioned in this, and in the other practice-related chapters, requires support. Unfortunately most social work agencies seem either unwilling or unable to offer this in the amount necessary for what can be a stressful and uncertain job, although supervision and consultation in groupwork is as necessary and essential as casework supervision (see Chapter 5). Even if expertise in groupwork is not available, then there is still a consultant role that can be offered. Many workers have found it helpful to have at least one 'external' person designated as consultant (regardless of the individual's expertise), who can offer an independent opinion both in preparing for a group and in discussing its operation.

In any of the situations that we have mentioned there are a variety of groupwork theories that could beneficially be considered by both workers and consultants. In particular, some models offer themselves for direct comparison, such as those concerned with a theory of the stages of group development. Tuckman (1965), Sarri and Galinsky (1967), and Whittaker (1970) all examine different ways in which stages of development can be attributed to groups. By using such theories it is possible to make direct comparisons between the stages of development in your group and that of the model. This can have two important effects: *(a)* it allows you to perceive behaviour as not being unique to your group, but perhaps of a type experienced by several other groups, and *(b)* it enables you to anticipate events that might happen in the future. An example of this is when fairly early in the group's life members often go through a period of challenging the leaders and generally being uncooperative – Tuckman's second phase of 'storming'. Being able to anticipate that this might happen can not only allow you to keep this confrontation in perspective, but it may also enable you to plan better strategies to cope with it. As Peter Smith (1978) writes:

> I find it helpful to think of the phases of group development . . . as a checklist of issues that are important in any group. Each may be emphasised or passed over lightly. An issue may be thoroughly explored at just one point in the group's history or returned to on many occasions.

Conclusion

The framework that we have discussed in this chapter is only one form of checklist. Another example is provided in Table 2.3. It was composed

Table 2.3 Significant incidents checklist

Problems	Yes	No
1. Have we booked the mini-bus?		
2. Have we informed all the social workers?		
3. Have we allowed enough time to collect and transport people?		
4. Have we worked out a recording system?		
5. Have we got a supervisor?		
6. Where are the keys to the hall kept?		
7. Have the leaders worked together before?		
8. Are the leaders agreed on the purpose of the group?		
9. Can the leaders get to each session?		
10. For how long do we intend the group to last?		
11. Do all group members know where and when to meet?		
12. Can we obtain a group consultant?		
13. Has our agency's management agreed to our proposal?		
14. What will happen to the members when the group ends?		
15. Have we got enough money?		

Problems	Yes	No
16. Is this really the right response to the expressed need?		
17. Do we know where all the equipment for the group is kept?		
18. Can the leaders meet to discuss the group after each session?		

in about ten minutes by the authors thinking of significant incidents that had gone wrong in groups they had run. The possibility of constructing a similar list is available to any worker contemplating setting up a group. While it covers some of the issues discussed in the main check-list, it can also help to cover some of the issues that might be peculiar to your agency or local situation. Such a system could be used in conjunction with the main list, or as an alternative to it; but whichever method is chosen, our point is a simple one: *Covering as many issues and problems as possible before a group starts is much more likely to leave energy and resources free to concentrate on the actual operation of the group.*

When the checklist that we have described in this chapter has been completed, then it only remains to consider finally the following points before starting the project:

(a)   Are you happy and comfortable with the group that you have constructed?

(b)   Have you avoided answering any of the questions?

(c)   Are you still sure that this group is the best possible means available for solving or coping with the expressed need?

3. Programme Planning

The previous chapter discussed some of the issues to be considered when structuring groups. It also stressed that groupwork is not synonymous with intermediate treatment, although working with groups of adolescents is likely to continue to be a major form of IT provision as the peer group is accepted to be a major influence on the adolescent. But what do you actually do with adolescents in the groups that are formed? And what alternatives are there to groupwork?

In this and the following chapter we explore some of the elements that might be included in an intermediate treatment programme for adolescents. In particular we attempt to offer some suggestions, and examples of exercises and approaches, which may be used when working with young people. However, before moving on to look at the content of IT programmes, it is necessary to make some general points about working with young people, and about relating programme design to the aims set for intervention.

The Medium is NOT the Message

A major reservation in writing about 'programming' is that it may be interpreted as offering a blueprint for timetabling contact and content with adolescents. If programming is seen as providing a list of events in some more or less desirable sequence, like the list of television and radio programmes which are timetabled in the *Radio Times*, then the discussion of programming is likely to be more restricting than illuminating. There is *no* right or wrong programme to follow religiously or discard, but there are certain techniques, events, and stimuli which may help us to move towards more effective contact with young people. However, these techniques and exercises are the means and not the ends of the work. The medium is therefore *not* the message.

The structure, format, and content of work with young people should not override the *process* of establishing a positive personal experience for that adolescent which is important to him at that point in time. It is the creation of encounters — within individuals, as well as between people — which is sought. The skill is to make these encounters positive and rewarding, rather than negative and destructive; to make them personal growth and change points, rather than confirming negative attitudes towards self and others. Sometimes it is during the ride home in the car, or while eating a meal together, that some of the most fruitful and honest discussions take place between adolescent and adult, and possibly this is because 'programme' (in the sense of a timetabled event or activity) is not detracting from the personal encounter which is taking place.

The skills in using this encounter are not planning techniques. Rather they are the interpersonal skills that have been identified by many researchers as leading to effective counselling. For instance, Truax and Carkhuff, in their review of research on this topic, identify what they call 'central therapeutic ingredients' within counselling. They state that 'research seems consistently to find empathy, warmth, and genuineness characteristics of human encounters that change people for the better', and they conclude that:

> Unless the parent or teacher is genuine in relating to a child, his warmth, caring and understanding have no meaning, or may even have a potentially threatening meaning. To be understood deeply or to receive a communication in a 'warm' voice can be deeply threatening if it comes from an unpredictable 'phoney' or a potential enemy. (Truax and Carkhuff, 1967)

Truax and Carkhuff offer some clues as to why intermediate treatment may be exhausting and threatening for social workers. Their suggestion is that effective work with young people requires the worker to meet the adolescent as another human being, not just as a 'delinquent' or 'deprived kid'. The role of social worker provides a mask behind which it is often easy to try and hide — thus maintaining a social and emotional distance between worker and client. Effective work, however, requires that the adult be willing to risk him*self* in the encounter with the adolescent; that he be willing to accept some of the difficulty and confusion that the young person may be experiencing. The greater the commitment of the worker to the adolescent, then the greater the strength of feeling he may experience.

This commitment to the adolescent, and knowledge of him, is likely to increase through the less formal contact that much intermediate treatment allows. Informality is appreciated by many clients as Sainsbury found during his consumer-focused research with Sheffield Family Service Unit:

> Preferences for particular workers were based on the following attributes, ranked in order of the frequency with which they were mentioned by clients:
> (i)   informality (homely, easy to talk to),
> (ii) getting close enough for honest discussions,
> (iii) patience,
> (iv) equal caring for everyone in the family,
> (v)   politeness.
> We have noted that clients chose factors relating to warmth of relationship and ethical integrity, and judged workers in these terms. Their regard for ethical factors and their relative disregard for efficiency in material matters were both underestimated by the caseworkers. (Sainsbury, 1975)

Sainsbury, like Truax and Carkhuff, stresses warmth within a relationship of integrity, caring, and personal encounter. This personal encounter was helped by an approach based on informality and openness. This is also echoed in Davies' research on the views of the consumers of a volunteer-based service for educationally subnormal school leavers in Manchester:

> The closer the volunteer approximated to a personal friend with whom the client could identify, the more enthusiastic were the attributes expressed. A particular illustration of this was the way in which families always mentioned instances when the volunteers had invited them to their own homes or had brought their husbands, wives, children or friends to the client's home: this action so clearly stamped the relationship with a strongly personal quality that it merited especial mention and almost always improved the image of the volunteer in the eyes of his client. Another element which crept in more than once was the assertion that 'she's not stuck up', 'she's easy to get on with'; despite the fact that, in many cases, the volunteer came from a cultural background that would normally have precluded her from access to the family's home on an informal basis, she was accepted and appreciated because of her approachable manner. This was a factor of some importance to many who compared the volunteer with social workers they had known and who had been less attentive and more distant in their manner. (Davies, 1977)

The lesson to be learnt is that it is not so much programme structure and content that determines the effectiveness of much intermediate treatment provision, but rather it is the attitudes and the interpersonal skills of the adults involved which are of primary importance. Ironically, many people in the community possess these attitudes and relationship skills, as is confirmed by Davies's research, but many social workers seem not to possess them.

Why Programming?

So why, if it is the relationship and awareness skills of the social worker that are often of primary importance in providing a relevant service for the adolescent, do we still continue to write about 'programming'?

There are two major reasons why programming is of importance. First, the encounter between social worker and adolescent does not take place spontaneously. It is not that social workers recruit their clients by walking down the street and just bumping into them by chance. The decision that the social worker and the client should meet is usually initially made by someone else (a parent, the school, the police, the courts). However, the social worker (and the client?) has some control over the settings in which they meet (home visits, office interviews, meetings over coffee in the cafe, etc.), and some locations may offer more scope for personal encounter than others. It is by trying to select the most satisfactory structure (venue, time) for meeting clients that the social worker may be able to facilitate these personal encounters.

So, some programmes of contact between worker and client may be more fruitful than others.

The second reason for programme planning is that not only do clients and social workers not meet spontaneously, but neither do they meet in a vacuum. There is a purpose, a goal, in them meeting together, and their contact is supposed to help achieve that aim. Therefore, in deciding upon appropriate methods of intervention, it is necessary to structure intervention in accordance with the aims to be achieved. With regard to intermediate treatment we now offer two models for conceptualizing and planning that structure and then consider some suggestions for *content* which might be included within the programmes.

Programme Planning

> We wish to stress that intermediate treatment is not synonymous with one particular method; a wide range of approaches and flexibility in using them is of essence. This enables the intermediate treatment worker to select the most appropriate 'tool' for the task. It should offer a federated approach, allowing the child or young person to participate in various forms of intermediate treatment in different settings – an acknowledgement of the fact that the needs of the young person are likely to vary over time and as his circumstances change. (Personal Social Services Council, 1977)

This statement from the Personal Social Services Council highlights the need for programmes of intermediate treatment to be broad and varied, so that the programmes are able to respond to the differing and changing needs of young people. For instance, in our present economic situation, with so many young people unemployed, programmes that offer opportunities for job creation (such as community workshops), or clubs open *during the day*, would seem to be a much needed form of provision. In some areas it may be that a major requirement is for programmes geared to minority ethnic groups, or for adolescents and their families who are being uprooted and moved to 'new town' housing estates. Local needs, which often reflect national social and economic trends, should be seen as determining factors when planning intermediate treatment provision.

At another level, cultural trends, or more accurately changes in style within working-class youth culture (e.g. from the mods and rockers, to skinheads, to punks), will also have their impact on the acceptability and appropriateness of programme content. Whether the programme should include opportunities for motor-bike maintenance, horse riding, 'banger racing', reggae discos, or rabbiting with ferrets, should depend on the embryo interests of the customers.

But intermediate treatment is not only about *interesting* adolescents in activities and hobbies. It is also about *influencing* their development, their attitudes, and their behaviour. Intermediate treatment is not a universal provision available to all young people; it is a selective provision which is to be made available to those who are seen to have particular unmet needs, or who are seen to be a nuisance to others.

So, how do we conceptualize a range of intermediate treatment provision? How do we plan a comprehensive framework of IT programmes?

Continuum of Care

Paley and Thorpe (1974) offer a 'continuum of care' as a framework for planning a range of programmes. The continuum model is based on the *intensity* of intervention that an adolescent receives. If he is seen to need a more intensive intervention in his life to reduce his offending or disturbance, he would be placed in a programme farther along the continuum than if his need for intervention were assessed to be minimal. For instance, he may simply benefit from supervision after school until his parents return home from work (a 'latchkey' club), or encouragement to relieve boredom by following a hobby or leisure interest. The aim is to move an adolescent from a programme on the continuum which is more intensive (including, for instance, day care and alternative schooling, and possibly manifest and specific behaviour modification techniques), towards the use of what Paley and Thorpe call 'basic and universal provisions', which might include youth clubs and other community resources, such as sports clubs. These basic facilities are available to the adolescent outside the intermediate treatment programme, and therefore will hopefully be used by him as a resource when his involvement in intermediate treatment ends. Fig. 3.1 illustrates a possible continuum of intermediate treatment programmes.

Treatment–Diversion Dichotomy

The continuum model is based upon varying intensities of intermediate treatment programmes, although it does not explicitly link programme design to aims. We can expand upon and clarify this model by relating it to our discussion of the aims of IT in Chapter 1 (see Table 1.1).

It is possible to argue that intermediate treatment provision could be conceptually divided between functions of diversion and treatment. With *diversion* (which is not being used here in the classical sense of diversion from the juvenile justice system *per se*; see Morris, 1978) the aim is to deflect the adolescent from involvement in delinquent, disturbing, and

Fig. 3.1

A possible continuum of intermediate treatment programmes

INTERMEDIATE TREATMENT

spontaneous use of basic and universal provisions, e.g. schools, youth clubs.	specialist youth club for the deprived and delinquent.	two/three evenings a week small group work with occasional residential periods.	day care and alternative schooling, with most week-ends residential.
referral to youth or community facilities.	once-a-week small group work.	evening and week-end care and supervision, with regular residential periods.	full-time residential care.

Increasing intensity of intervention ➤

◄ Desired direction of movement of any individual

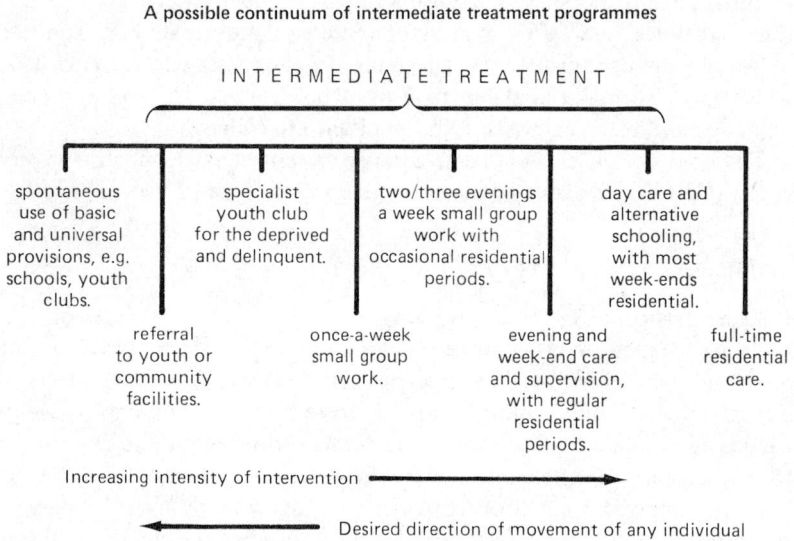

SOURCE: Based on Paley and Thorpe (1974), p. 86.

difficult behaviour by offering equally rewarding and satisfying distractions. There is no necessary assumption here that the adolescent is disturbed, abnormal, or that he needs treatment to change him. It is his behaviour, and particularly his use of leisure, which is the problem, and it is at the level of his behaviour, rather than, for instance, his personality and attitudes, that the diversion programme would be aimed. The programme might include youth club provision, community service components, or the stimulation of hobbies and interests which are not seen as troublesome by others.

However, the *treatment* aims of intermediate treatment make assumptions that the adolescent is disturbed or abnormal in some way. The aim of the intervention, therefore, is to treat and remedy the disturbance. This may be a result, for example, of emotional trauma within the adolescent's family, or of personal abnormality, such as hyperactivity resulting from brain damage. However, treatment might also mean the correcting of deviant or unhelpful learned behaviour, where delinquency becomes a habit because it has been rewarded in the past through status or material gain.

The aims of intermediate *treatment* include compensating for the deprivation and trauma that the adolescent may have experienced by offering him rewarding, caring, and consistent relationships, particularly with adults, and opportunities to increase his self-esteem and change his self-image. The aims might also include challenging and confronting his troublesome behaviour, and the offering of alternative behaviours which are then rewarded by the adults and peers within the intermediate treatment programme.

Fig. 3.2 presents the treatment – diversion dichotomy as another continuum, and suggests possible programme content for points upon it. In reality the split between treatment – diversion is false as any programme may include a focus on treatment *and* diversion strategies, but this continuum should help us to sharpen our thinking about the aims *and* means of our programmes.

Fig. 3.2

Treatment—diversion dichotomy and programme planning

FOCUS	FOCUS
Reduce deprivation	Tackle deviance
Preventive rather than reactive	Reactive rather than preventive
Social orientation rather than	Personal orientation rather than
personal orientation	social orientation
Adolescent as normal	Adolescent as abnormal

DIVERSION ⊢————————————————————⊣ TREATMENT

hobbies	practical	social	attitude	behaviour
fun	skills	skills	exploration	confrontation
entertainment	and knowledge	training		and
				modification

(possible programme content)

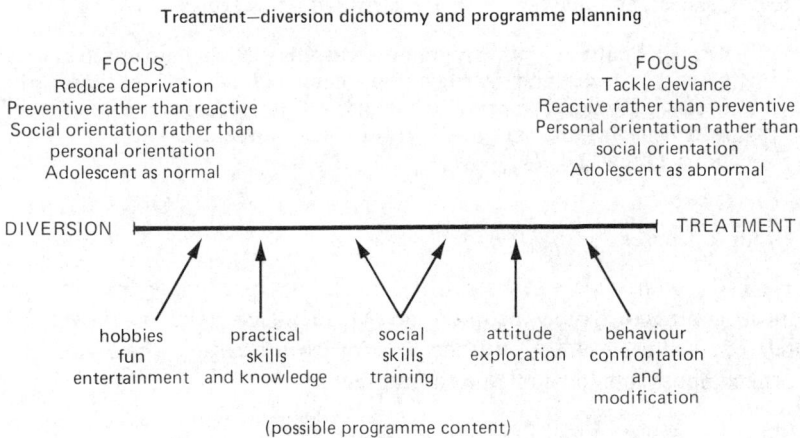

Programme Content

Having discussed some ways of thinking about over-all programme planning, we now look at the content that might be included within the programmes. We focus on a limited number of techniques and exercises that we have found useful in our work with adolescents, and then look in more detail at the use of residential experiences within intermediate treatment and at the provision of more intensive programmes of IT.

Before we describe and comment on some actual exercises which we have used with young people we would again wish to emphasize the warnings given earlier. Programmes cannot be neatly and rigidly determined in advance, and the real impact of our work is still likely to be in the relationship which we establish with the adolescent. This is accepted wisdom within parts of the youth service:

> The fact is that any adult who attempts to determine the setting of his work simply by defining beforehand a kind of group experience which will enable him to be helpful to young people must very seriously handicap his social–educational practice. Such predetermination fails to allow for the real complexity and changeability of human relationships and for the variety of individual experience derived from them, and thus needlessly blinkers a social educator's attitude towards his work. (Davies and Gibson, 1967).

We would also want to warn against the reaction identified by Macalister Brew that anything others suggest might be all right for them, but it is never all right for ourselves — often because we are not willing to take the plunge and try something different from the safe and trusted table tennis, soccer, and maybe a little cooking and a few trips:

> The difficulty about programme planning is that no matter what activity or method is suggested there will always be those who declare, 'It can't be done in our group'. Indeed one is often forced into believing that all youth groups work under a Statute of Limitations. (Brew, 1957)

Group Exercises

We list below some exercises which might be appropriate for use with most groups of young people (and we reference more extensively to related further reading), but the decision to use any of these exercises or techniques should be related to four factors:

(a)   The aims of the programme.
(b)   The intensity of the programme.
(c)   The abilities and the confidence of the adolescents.
(d)   The stage of group development (see p. 36), and of the development of relationships between individuals (peer–peer; peer–adult; adult–adult).

Fig. 3.3 relates the stages of group development to possible programme content, and the figure also suggests that the more intensive the programme, and the more frequent the contact with the adolescents, then the quicker the group is likely to move through the earlier stages of group development. It is also true that the more intensive the programme, the sooner it is likely to end, as intensive programmes are usually planned for limited periods only. This partly reflects the idea that short-term intensive work is likely to be more effective than long-term, low-key work, but it might also reflect the reality that social worker stamina and agency resources are limited.

Fig. 3.3

Stages of group development, possible programme content, and
the relationship with the intensity of the programme

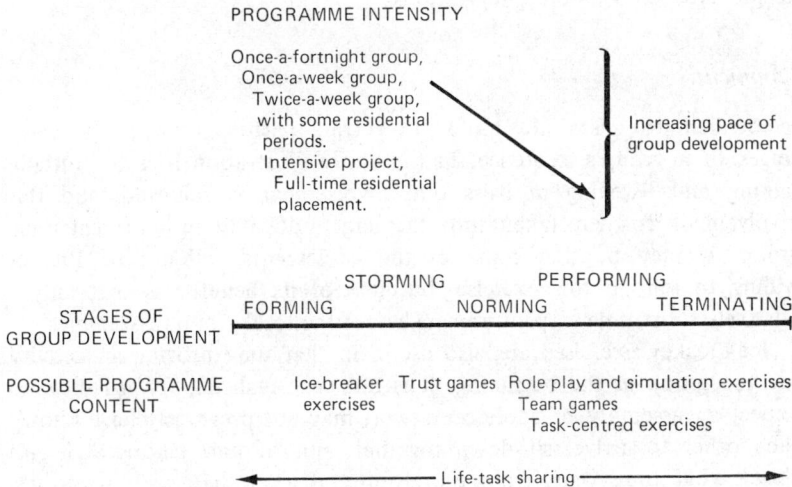

PROGRAMME INTENSITY

Once-a-fortnight group,
Once-a-week group,
Twice-a-week group,
with some residential
periods.
Intensive project,
Full-time residential
placement.

Increasing pace of
group development

	STORMING	PERFORMING	
	FORMING	NORMING	TERMINATING

STAGES OF
GROUP DEVELOPMENT

POSSIBLE PROGRAMME
CONTENT

Ice-breaker
exercises

Trust games

Role play and simulation exercises
Team games
Task-centred exercises

Life-task sharing

Ice-breaker Exercises

Aims:

To help members of a new group to relax, to get to know each other, and
to set the tone of a sharing and caring group; to minimize inclusion problems in a group when some, but not all, members know each other; to
emphasize *listening* as well as *talking.*

Illustration:

'My friend likes . . .'. Get the group to split into pairs and for one person
to ask the other about the things he likes. After a couple of minutes get
the pairs to reverse roles, so that the other person is then asked about the
things he likes.

The total group then reassembles, and each person is asked to tell the
group about the things his friend likes. He is asked to start by saying 'My
friend John (or whatever his partner was called) likes . . .'.

Group members can then explore further with each other the things
that they have said that they like (e.g. somebody likes soccer; does anybody play in a football team? Does anybody go to watch soccer?).

This exercise can also lead into a discussion about the group, what the members would like to do in the group, and what interests or activities they would like to follow up. During this time the adults can also be introducing a discussion of ground rules for the group – Who is going to do the work to arrange certain activities? How is the group to decide between competing suggestions?

Comment:

Ice-breaker exercises are useful in getting participation in the early stages of a group's existence. In the above illustration it is by initially talking and listening in pairs that involvement is achieved, and this involvement is then taken into the larger, possibly more threatening, group. It may be that some of the adolescents will not be able or willing to join in this exercise, but one of its benefits is that only a relatively short time is spent in pairs before the total group reassembles.

Ice-breaker exercises are also useful in that they provide an activity for the group at the beginning. It is not very realistic, for instance, to expect an assembly of adolescents who may not previously have known each other to arrive, sit down together, and to start talking at length about what they want from the group and what they want to do. As one social worker said when talking about a group which never really got going, 'We should have had positive ideas to start with. There was a lag of five or six weeks before getting started.' The positive ideas that are needed may not necessarily be a list of activities which the group will undertake, but it may be some ideas of exercises to get the participation and commitment of the adolescents in the group's formation stage (see Pfeiffer and Jones).

Trust Games

Aims:

To help to increase the cohesion of the group and commitment of the members to each other.

Illustration:

Get the group to stand in a circle so that they can touch the body of the person on either side of them. One person stands within the circle which the group forms and closes his eyes. This person then holds himself rigid and falls backwards into the arms of one of the people

in the circle. This person then rocks the person forward so that he is standing upright again. The person within the circle then falls backwards into the arms of the next person in the circle, and so on until he has been passed around the group. (This exercise is shown in the Department of Health and Social Security's film *Intermediate Treatment in Action*.)

Variations on this theme could include being led around blindfolded, or even being pushed around in a wheelchair, where you remain dependent on another person and where you put yourself at some risk.

Comment:

Trust games, like the suggestions above, test out and reinforce the confidence that group members have in each other. It is important that they are well led and supervised as there is an element of physical as well as emotional risk attached to these exercises. If not well supervised they could become the medium for scapegoating and bullying.

An advantage of exercises which require physical contact is that they offer explicit opportunities for non-verbal communication. For some of our adolescents this may be an important consideration. However, others will also be unhappy and threatened by some 'touch exercises', as in some physical encounter programmes, which seem to them to be unnatural (e.g. touching and exploring each other's faces). Cries of 'he's queer' are likely to be followed by more intensive attempts to disrupt and deflect from this type of threatening experience, and it may be more appropriate to avoid exercises which seem unnatural to the adolescents (see Button, 1974, pp. 81–3).

Role Play

Aims:

To help to focus on an issue; to explore alternative reactions and solutions to problems; to explore attitudes; and to increase awareness.

Illustration:

One lad in an intermediate treatment group was to appear in court charged with theft. It was suggested to the group by the adults that the group should write a paragraph for the social enquiry report on their picture of the lad. What did they feel should happen to him when he appeared in court? How should he plead? What should he say?

The group role played the court hearing. One of the adults took the key

role of Clerk to the Magistrates so that the hearing was conducted as realistically as possible. Other roles were chosen by the adolescents and remaining adults.

The role play:

(a) crossed a threshold by allowing the adolescents and adults to talk about their situation, experiences, and anxieties,

(b) made this talking and thinking fun,

(c) provided a forum for teaching the adolescents about the mechanism of the juvenile court and juvenile justice,

(d) involved as participants even those who were normally very much 'outside' our discussions,

(e) gave the adults further understanding about the perceptions and concerns of the adolescents. For example, the adolescents held to an adversary rather than welfare model of the juvenile court, but accepted the justice of differential sentencing. In the role play one of the defendants was sentenced to three months at a detention centre as 'he was older and should have known better', while the other defendant received a three-year conditional discharge and a £20 fine as 'he was younger and did a paper round'. Both the sentences were punishment- rather than treatment-centred.

Comment:

Role play can be used to focus on issues within the group (like an incident of theft from the group's premises); it can be used to explore personal issues for individuals (like a pending court appearance, or arguments at home); or it can be used to anticipate difficulties the adolescents might experience (like going for a job interview, or being goaded into shoplifting by mates).

Role play is initially threatening, but it is also exciting. The commitment of the participants is likely to increase during the role play (but do not leave too many people hanging around for too long as observers as they will soon get bored and disruptive), and their contributions will often be very honest and therefore emotionally very important to them. The responses from the adults should be caring and interested. It is better to ask questions if someone seems to be wrongly playing their role than to deny outright the reality of the role as they see it.

Role play can require preparation (for instance, it may be necessary to get the adolescents to talk about the roles before playing them, as they may find certain roles difficult because they cannot identify with, or have no experience of, them), and it certainly needs time to be allowed for

discussion and exploration of the attitudes and perceptions expressed within the role play. It is particularly important that if, for example, the role play is about an incident of delinquency, that it does not become another opportunity for the adolescents to boast about their exploits without being questioned on what it feels like to be in court and to be worried about being 'sent away'; how their parents feel when they get in trouble; or why they take risks in the first place. Some of this questioning should occur within the role play, rather than being left to the end when the adolescents may lose interest and want to move on to something else. Button (1974, pp. 91–7) offers further comment on role play with adolescents.

Team Games and Task-centred Exercises

Aims:

To get the group to work together, and to explore through discussion how the group is working, and the parts played by individuals within it. Successful performance of the team or completion of the task, especially if there is a material product at the end, helps to enhance self-esteem and status.

Illustration:

Apart from the obvious examples, like a football team, there are tasks which a group can undertake for its own benefit (like making a table-tennis table) or for the benefit of others (like the shop index described on p. 77).

Comment:

Team games and task-centred exercises can help to confirm the solidarity of the group, especially by competing, for instance, against other groups. They can also heighten and make more obvious the conflicts and schisms within the group. In a football team which one of us ran, one lad rarely received a pass from anyone on his side. It was not that he was a bad footballer (he wasn't), but he was an isolate and a scapegoat within the group. When this team lost (our usual fate!) the discord within the group was well illustrated by one faction blaming another and occasionally kicking-out against the opposition.

We have suggested that team games and task-centred exercises might be successfully undertaken if they occur at the 'performing stage' of group development, but they can also be introduced to get the group to explore issues of its own performance at earlier stages. As with all these exercises, it is the opportunities that they present for focusing on personal and group issues which is as important as any rewards they give to participants in their own right.

Life-task Sharing

Aims:

To get the group to share responsibility; and to allow individuals to be fully involved in the life of the group.

Illustration:

Many groups provide, for instance, coffee and biscuits during group meetings, and need to tidy the meeting place at the end of the session. During residential periods meals need to be cooked. Activities and events have to be planned and arranged, and when group members are absent it may be appropriate to visit them to check that they are not ill, or that they have not been upset by something which happened at the group. In many groups the adults take on, and see through, all these responsibilities. It gives the adults a definite leadership and controlling role within the group, and the adolescents are often more like consumers of pre-arranged activities than full participants in the life of the group.

Comment:

It may be easier, and less time-consuming, for the adults to undertake all the planning and organizational tasks for the group, but it robs the adolescents of the opportunity to feel responsible for, and involved in, what is happening to them. It also takes away from them natural opportunities to learn to use the telephone or to write letters when they help to arrange trips or camps. In addition it deprives the adults of the opportunity to allocate tasks so that isolates and scapegoats can be more integrated into the group.

For instance, in one group a boy who was isolated and seen as irresponsible and untrustworthy by the other adolescents, volunteered to get the biscuits and milk for the group from the shop each week. This made him a central member of the group at coffee times, when the other group members had to approach him and ask him for their biscuits.

In another group a lad who disrupted any planning discussions was given the role of treasurer. He had to keep an account of the expenditure of the group, and to report to the members on the state of their budget. After the group ended this adolescent, along with others in his group, was interviewed to find out what he felt about the group. He spoke at some length, and with much enthusiasm, about his important and responsible role within the group.

It is not suggested that getting adolescents to take part in the chores of the groups is an easy option. Far from it! Few people like to be doing the washing-up while others are playing football or sitting around talking. But the failure of some people to take their part in the less exciting, but still necessary, aspects of the life of the group can provide a focus for some of the discussions with the adolescents about the performance of the group, and of the attitudes of its members.

Individual Skill Development

So far we have focused on some possible approaches to working with adolescent groups, and we have suggested some exercises which might be used with the groups. But we would again stress that intermediate treatment is not just about small groupwork, and we now look briefly at two forms of programme content that might be offered to adolescents outside of groups, although they are relevant to group programmes as well.

Learning Practical Skills

Aims:

To offer opportunities to learn a practical skill which might be of use to the adolescent's life now and as an adult. The acquisition of the skill may also enhance self-esteem, and provide a source of praise from others.

Illustration:

The practical skills might include, for instance, learning to fish (which could provide a leisure interest now and as an adult), carpentry, or car mechanics (which again offer immediate satisfaction and long-term rewards). The skills could be taught by a volunteer, as with the fishing club described in Table 2.1 in Chapter 2. It may be that the adolescent could be linked with clubs and associations in the community which share an interest in the activity. If the practice of the skill, for example gardening, provides a useful material end-product (e.g. home-grown vegetables), then this can be used to enhance the adolescent's status within his family and among his friends.

Comment:

The learning of a useful skill is beneficial in its own right, but it also gives opportunities for the adolescent to be linked with a caring adult through the medium of a shared interest. It is important that if the adolescent does acquire an interest in a particular skill or hobby, that it is ensured that he has the means to continue with this activity outside of any formal intermediate treatment programme. It may be necessary, for instance, to buy him a fishing-rod or to link him with a fishing club which is willing to assist him.

It may be assumed that the encouragement of practical skills and interests takes place at school, and that therefore this is not really a relevant area for intermediate treatment. However, some adolescents are so alienated from school that they do not take advantage of the opportunities available to them, and they only intensify their own disadvantage. For other adolescents it may be that because of their reputation the school excludes them from opportunities which are available to other children. For example, the following quotation is taken from a research report on the consumers' views of one intermediate treatment group:

> It seemed particularly unfortunate that the lad from a single parent family, who had been left a lathe when his grandfather died, was not allowed to do woodwork at school. There apparently was not enough space in the woodwork workshop for all the people in his class. His mother was 'thoroughly disgusted' about it.

(White and Brockington, 1978, offer some comments and suggestions on 'survival skills' which relate to both practical and social skill training.)

Social Skill Training

Aims:

To improve the adolescents' ability to deal with issues and tasks within their own lives by practising and rehearsing problem-solving techniques, and by learning some skills of everyday living.

Illustration:

A source of conflict for many adolescents is their relationship with adults. They experience adults as restricting, and they respond with argumentative and confrontational behaviour. This behaviour may result in further difficulties, and may even lead to them taking action which puts them at risk of offending and being exploited (e.g. running away from home). By getting the adolescent to list those issues which often lead him into disputes with adults, by exploring with him the causes of these disputes, and by rehearsing with him alternative responses that he can make when these issues arise, it may be possible to help him to handle disagreements in a way which is less hurtful, and more helpful to him.

Comment:

Social skills training can help the adolescent to handle existing crises in his life more successfully, to anticipate future difficulties, and to practise and rehearse behaviours which increase his repertoire of responses to problems. It involves the individual in identifying difficulties that he experiences and then working out for himself possible solutions to these problems. Much social skills training is accomplished through the use of participative exercises, and this offers the advantage of increasing the commitment and involvement of the individual within the programme. (See Priestley *et al.*, 1978, for a very useful guide to social skills training.)

The Residential Experience

This section does not deal, as might be suggested by the title, with intermediate treatment in residential centres, but instead covers the implications of using a residential experience as part of a programme for community-based groups. The reason for not looking at residential centres in detail is mainly one of limited space, although hopefully several of the issues raised here (and elsewhere in the book) will be found relevant to those working in that field.

We have already mentioned in Chapter 2 (see p. 30) that the addition of residential periods to a groupwork project can accelerate the processes of development within the group. However, adding a residential component to any IT programme has implications beyond group development, and this section endeavours to cover these under the headings of planning, leadership, and the emotional impact of the residential experience.

Planning

As for the whole programme, the importance of pre-planning is vital in achieving a successful residential experience. Among the questions to be answered are 'Is the "trip" part of the "treats" aspect of the group?', and 'When are such residential breaks to occur?'. In thinking about the latter question, then any acceptance of the ideas surrounding 'a stages of group development theory' will indicate that the timing of such an experience can be crucial. You may wish to use the event at the start of a programme so as to accelerate the 'getting to know you phase', or alternatively, towards the end, so that more time can be allowed for the group to achieve and accomplish its goals.

Moving from the general to the specific, consideration will need to be given to questions such as 'Who is going to plan and obtain food?' and 'Who is going to be responsible for parts or all of the programme?'. Groups run haphazardly on a once-a-week basis have the unhappy tendency to get even worse when a residential experience is attempted.

Planning includes deciding where to go . . .

Q)   Is it really necessary, in order to present new experiences to group members, to spend six hours travelling half-way across the country, when those adolescents' previous experience has only been very limited and local?

. . . and the kind of venue at which you wish to stay:

Q)   Do those funny little marks on the Ordnance Survey map mean that the field in which you are planning to camp is meadow or marshy ground?

Q)   Does the rather vague section in the Adventure Centre brochure mean that you are supposed to take your own Calor gas supplies, or will they be provided? Oh, and you are willing to take part in all the activities that they are providing, aren't you?

Q)   Has the youth hostel you are about to use been visited by another group from your agency, and, if so, did they experience any problems?

In addition to the problems of physical planning, allowing an appropriate amount of time to do things, and catering for your group members' previous experience, are also issues to be considered. Cooking and washing-up after a meal takes a lot longer when tackled in the pouring rain behind a tent flap than when done with a modern hot water heater and sink. Explaining to the group members why cooking a roast chicken on a camping stove is not really on can entail problems and take time!

To cope with some of the issues that we have mentioned, the worker(s) can adopt a range of tactics. There are practical measures to be considered, such as if this is the first time that leaders and members alike have used tents, then a practice 'putting up' session is helpful if you wish to avoid deciphering instructions translated from Korean on a dark and windswept piece of moorland. Discussion can be helpful to determine whether the rules and boundaries of the group are adequate to cope with new situations with which you are all about to be confronted. Finally, before commencing your journey, it might also be advisable for the workers to contemplate various difficulties that can arise, and possibly to role play responses to them. While this may sound unduly pessimistic, many groups encounter similar problems, and having some sort of response ready can be of great assistance. Typical of these are: the mini-bus breaking down on an isolated stretch of road; people getting bored and restless during the journey; one member of the group being exceptionally difficult to control; one person being bullied by the others; a group of individuals 'going off' and not returning to the pre-arranged pick-up point. All of these situations pose threats or problems to the leaders, and a preparatory session could be used to discover potential reactions and solutions before the incidents occur.

Leadership

The residential experience can be a testing, but also satisfying, event for the group leaders. It can exacerbate or accentuate problems encountered in the community or during the non-residential meetings of the group, or alternatively, it may raise new issues. Either way, there are many methods by which the worker can attempt to overcome potential problems once they have been recognized.

If Leader A has already had substantial disagreements with Leader B over worker-style or method of leadership within the group, then it is important to resolve these disputes before going into residence. It is here that the use of a consultant can be particularly helpful. The failure to establish common goals, or unity of purpose, is much more likely to be revealed and exploited when the group is together twenty-four hours a day than at any other time. Brian Truckle and Elizabeth Schardt outline some of the issues of co-leadership in an adolescent group:

> It is of great benefit to be able to share the responsibility and duties involved in running a group, but this does involve very important work on the relationship between the counsellors. Counsellors must be able to work as a team and to know their own 'modus vivendi' and that of their colleagues, and thus be able to work out difficulties between them, preferably outside the group. Conflicts that happen between them in the group can be used constructively when both counsellors are really 'en rapport' with one another. It cannot be too greatly stressed that the relationship between the co-therapists needs both time and effort to help it become an effective therapeutic tool. Emotionally disturbed children are very quick to pick up any relationship difficulty between the counsellors, such as who in fact is being the 'best parent', who does the caring and/or limit setting role. (Truckle and Schardt, 1975)

If we accept that workers often feel threatened and slightly unsure of their role when working in any kind of adolescent group setting for the first time, then the residential experience, with its intensive contact, must represent the height of that anxiety. There are a variety of ways in which such worries can either be tackled well, or conversely, avoided with damaging consequences. Timetabling the experience until such a time as the workers feel able to cope with a more intensive experience is one way of handling the issue. However, a more common response is that the workers retreat during the residential experience into becoming domestics, and use up a vast amount of time in maintaining premises, cooking food, and clearing-up, so that very little time is left for actual face-to-face contact with each other or with the adolescents. While this is often rationalized by saying that it is 'much easier and less time-consuming to do such tasks yourself', if the notion of a *group* experience has any meaning then surely it is a situation where all the members are equally and actively involved. Apart from this, the task of completing chores together encourages feelings such as mutual responsibility, as well as being an important time when one-to-one communication can take place.

We mentioned above rehearsing potential problem situations before they arise. In discussions with workers, one in particular is often aired: the 'late night ritual'. The scenario goes as follows:

(a) Workers and members alike have had an exhausting and demanding first day exploring the new situation in which they find themselves.
(b) Group members go to bed, however, still fairly 'high' and excited by the events that have occurred.
(c) Group leaders go to bed extremely tired and drained by the new experience.
(d) Members continue to create an amount of disturbance and disruption which threatens to continue throughout the night.

The situation that is now left is potentially explosive. The group members are wondering 'how far they can push their luck', and the leaders are considering whether they can keep their tempers, whether another leader should intervene, or whether if they turn over in their beds/sleeping-bags the disturbance will gradually just fade away. Some of the ways of avoiding this situation are:

(a) To arrange an exercise that releases tension or calms the group before going to bed. This might include, for instance, a fairly tranquil camp fire and barbecue.
(b) To attempt to achieve a state of physical tiredness, especially on the first night away. This might include playing a night wide-game.
(c) To threaten a midnight walk if the noise continues. Only make

this threat if you are willing to carry it out. Why not organize a midnight hike in the first place anyway?

(d) To use your own charisma to instil some calm and order, to use your sense of dramatic presence in appealing to the group's better nature ('come on, lads, I'm knackered after driving the mini-bus'), and to remember that it is not abnormal, or particularly depraved and deviant, for the kids to be larking around into the early hours of the morning. Obviously there is more scope to tolerate their noise if they are not disturbing any others outside of your group, and this should be born in mind when planning your residential location.

(e) Never lose your temper (although it is often appropriate to express anger), as once you have over-reacted and 'blown your top' you have probably escalated the incident and have forced yourself and the adolescents into opposing corners.

In discussing leadership in this context, as in any context, useful tips and ideas can be acquired from many sources. Other social workers, youth leaders, teachers, and particularly residential workers, probably all have some hints to offer.

Emotional Content

As suggested above, there is a strong emotional content in working with groups which is heightened when you share a residential experience. Indeed, this heightening of the emotional experience is one of the rationales for the residential period.

For the social worker, it enables him to demonstrate that he is a 'normal' human being. While it can hardly be a source of great surprise to the adolescent to find that social workers also curse when they hit their thumb with a mallet, or that they clean their teeth in a particular way, it does help to establish the social worker as a 'real' person. Spontaneous caring, frustration, and anger can be demonstrated, which is much more relevant and real than just talking about emotions and feelings. This is not to say that the 'talk' element should be abandoned, but that it is enhanced by being related to immediate and shared experiences. This often makes the social worker–client relationship more significant for both of them.

One consequence of the residential experience is that it allows some adolescents to regress because of the relative security offered by the relationship that they have with the adults, and because they are away from the pressures and tensions of home. For example, during a camping week-end a 15-year-old, who was one of the toughest boys in the group (his last offence had been for inflicting grievous bodily harm), drew comments from the workers on his behaviour. This consisted of running in and out of the sea and feeling the waves with his hands. When he was asked what he was doing he replied quite simply that he was playing! Bearing in mind his status as the eldest child in a family which had an absent father, the opportunities for carefree play in his childhood had probably been few and far between. As well as being a sign of the trust already established between the social worker and the adolescent, acceptance of this type of behaviour without mocking or ridicule furthers the caring and the sharing between them.

Similar opportunities are offered when someone is homesick. Sympathetic responses, a willingness to allow the adolescent to spend time with you, allowing opportunities to talk about home, assisting the adolescent to be diverted into other activities, and helping him place the period that he is away from home into some time perspective (by, for instance, drawing with him a calendar of the time he is away, marking on it events that are planned during this period, and getting him to tick off days – even half days – as they pass) help to show that you recognize and accept the feelings he has and that you care about them.

The emotional content of a residential experience can express itself in a variety of ways, not all of which are easy to understand or interpret while they are actually happening. Initially the group may revert to the early stages of its existence with new alliances being formed among the members. There may also be a strong identification of wherever you are staying as 'our place', which can result in destructive behaviour when leaving, as though the members do not wish anyone else to desecrate what was felt to be theirs. Certainly leaving can be a difficult time, combining what is sometimes an understandable reluctance to return home with wishes that the experience of being together could continue 'for ever'.

The checklist (Table 3.1) covers several of the issues mentioned in this section that you may need to cover before 'going away'.

Planning Intensive Projects

> We believe that a considerable number of young people who are at present committed to some form of institutional care would be better dealt with in the community. We therefore propose that an intensive form of intermediate treatment should be adopted. . . . It is envisaged that this programme, to be developed within the framework of intermediate treatment provision as a requirement of a supervision order, will offer an intensive form of care for those more heavily involved in delinquent activities who can be contained within the community, and who are able to live with their own families. (Personal Social Services Council, 1977)

Table 3.1 A checklist for residential experiences

Who is getting the food?
Who is arranging the transport?
Have you planned particular activities while you are away?
Who is going to lead them?
Have you made yourself well acquainted with where you are going?
Have you questioned or thought about the relationship between the leaders?
Have you all considered responses to potential problems? . . . emotional, e.g. bullying, isolates. physical, e.g. bad weather, transport failing.
Have you told parents?
Have you obtained consent forms from parents?
Are you using guides for particular activities, e.g. canoeing?
Have you checked their qualifications and experience?
Have you sorted out the leadership relationship with them?
If you are staying at an established centre or hostel, have you sorted out your leadership roles with the resident staff?
Are the adults going to take part in all the activities with adolescents?
Have you left clear instructions about your location with a responsible person from your agency?
Do parents know how to contact you?
Have you got a first-aid kit?
Have you got a map of the area?
Do you know about local hospitals (casualty departments)?
Are you all insured?

The Personal Social Services Council's report on intermediate treatment had as one of its main proposals the provision of 'intensive' intermediate treatment. It offered a model which included an initial two-week residential component to allow the adolescent to be assessed, and also to register with him and his family that 'he is to participate in a deliberate and planned programme which will aim to meet his needs and to reduce his involvement in anti-social behaviour'. The residential period would be followed by a daily programme which might include work experience, community service, and an educational component which encourages the adolescent to look at his personal situation. This intensive provision would be provided within a framework in which 'the responsibilities of the young person, his family, the supervisor, and the project staff should be clearly understood'.

The proposals of the Personal Social Services Council are similar to two of the more intensive stages identified by Paley and Thorpe on their continuum of IT:

Stage 7 – Local treatment group. Highly intensive supervision and family casework by specialist social workers. Three nights a week, and three week-ends out of four. Night stay facilities and block residential periods. Work with parallel parents groups. . . .

Stage 9 – Day care. Highly intensive supervision and family casework. Educational provision on a free school model. Specialist staff include teachers and trade instructors as well as social workers. Work with parallel parents group. (Paley and Thorpe, 1974)

For local authorities intensive projects can present a highly viable option, being less intensive (and less costly) than residential care, remaining community based, and yet being distinctly different from, and offering much more than, one-to-one and family-based supervision. If this is so, then the question remains as to why intensive projects are rarely initiated. The explanation that we would offer (and to which we return in Chapter 6) is that local authorities give the strong impression of planning by adaptation from existing provision, rather than planning from need. For most departments this existing provision was mainly office-based supervision and residential care. The next step, therefore, was the development of one-session-per-week groups which were run by the caseworkers, and short-stay residential centres. The intensive project lies between these two starting-points, and is therefore likely to be the last to be provided.

We give below an example of a fairly intensive programme based on the original outline of a project that was led by one of the authors. It attempted to provide a fairly structured experience in terms of its referral procedure and its daily programme. By using contracts and review meetings it sought to involve parents in an analysis of the adolescent's difficulties and in the operation of the project:

Outline of One Intensive Project

Purpose:

To avoid the adolescent being received into care; and to provide a resource for children being returned home from care.

Age and Sex:

Boys and girls with a functioning age of between 12 and 16.

Project Operation:

The project will be at the IT Centre and will operate from 3.30 p.m. to 7.30 p.m. on Wednesdays, Thursdays, and Fridays. The project is planned to last for one year. The length of stay with the project for any adolescent will depend on his/her contract of referral. All will be expected to attend each session of the project during their period of involvement with it.

Programme:

Each evening will be divided into four sections; these can be altered with the agreement of the project staff and the adolescents.

3.30–4.30 free introductory activity – table tennis, TV, cards, chess, other indoor games, records.
4.30–5.15 meal – to be prepared by the staff and adolescents.
5.15–7.00 structured, individually chosen, activity period, which is likely to involve instructors – pottery, building, decorating, crafts; individual skill instruction (e.g. reading).
7.00–7.30 community meeting – notes to be taken alternatively by adolescents and adults, and to be available to all on the following day.

Criteria for Acceptance:

(a) That the adolescent is nearing reception into care.
(b) That the adolescent agrees to attend.
(c) That the person legally responsible for the adolescent agrees to his/her attendance.
(d) That it is physically feasible for the adolescent to attend (e.g. distance from home, degree of any physical handicap).
(e) That a contract of admission has been established.

Initial Contract Meeting:

The purpose of this meeting is to:

(a) introduce the adolescent and his/her parents to the project,
(b) form a contract between the person legally responsible for the adolescent, the adolescent and the project.

The discussion should centre on why the adolescent is close to being received into care, what problems could occur that would necessitate reception into care, and how the project could prevent those problems occurring or help to resolve them. At the end of the meeting it is hoped that a contract will be agreed, and that it will cover the following points:

(a)   Why the adolescent was referred to the project.
(b)   How the project might help.
(c)   What is expected of all the parties to the contract.
(d)   The frequency of review dates.
(e)   The date of discharge from the project (length of stay would not be expected to exceed six months).

Review Meetings:

These should be held to determine whether the five points of the original contract need alteration. The contract can only be altered if the original parties attend and agree.

Additional reviews can be called if the adolescent, parent(s), case-workers, or project staff feel that immediate reception into care is necessary, or that the adolescent should end his contract with the project.

Staffing:

Two full-time staff, plus craft instructors.

Adolescent Numbers:

A maximum of six at any one time.

As the project developed a number of issues emerged. Firstly, the project began to move away from its formal structured programme. This was partly because there were never more than four adolescents involved with the project at any one time, which created an atmosphere more akin to a therapeutic community, or even a family, than a task-centred environment. Secondly, the project never achieved enough involvement with the families to keep pace with some of the problems that the adolescents were facing. This meant that they were still likely to be received into care as a result of circumstances beyond the project's influence. Thirdly, despite many attempts to make clear the boundaries of responsibility between the project staff and caseworkers, confusion still occurred. Fourthly, the commitment of the project workers to the adolescents grew during the project, and the project tended to become more of a 'haven' for the adolescents from the problems that they were experiencing, instead of it operating as a 'problem solving agency'.

These are only a few of the issues that this project raised, and some are similar to Waterhouse's (1978) description and analysis of another fairly intensive project. Waterhouse found that while the staff were not unfamiliar with working with adolescents, they had little experience in the specific kind of group setting that they had structured. In particular, there was some difficulty in applying concepts of democracy and participation in practice. It was suggested that these problems would have been lessened if the workers had defined their objectives more clearly, and if they had established a contract in the beginning with each adolescent. Waterhouse also found some confusion between 'talking' and 'doing', and he suggested that this could have been clarified by distinguishing between 'activity as an end in itself', 'activity as a means to an end', and 'focused discussion'.

Several of the issues raised by these descriptions of two fairly intensive projects have already been examined in Chapter 2; for example, the need to define and be precise about purpose and objectives. Waterhouse's description and analysis also highlights the pressure that can be put on leaders of groups: 'Group workers' authority was openly challenged and genuine responses were expected to questions about personal attitudes and experiences' (Waterhouse, 1978).

Such issues have a tendency to become even more significant when the frequency of contact is increased, and we now briefly look at some of these issues in relation to intensive projects.

Contracts

The process of establishing a contract, particularly within the framework of a referral or admission meeting, can be crucial in understanding why a particular adolescent needs to attend the project. Sometimes this initial meeting can become a therapeutic opportunity in its own right, when, for instance, the adolescent is close to being received into care. By focusing on the person legally responsible for the adolescent it can help to restore authority to parents or a social worker where that authority may have been lacking. Such a session, therefore, serves to clarify problems and issues, as well as helping to make the adolescent's attendance at the project both understandable and understood. Faith Raven (1973) discusses the usefulness of this type of admission procedure with regard to a residential adolescent unit.

Programme

Considerable thought needs to be given in planning a programme for an intensive project. In using activities a distinction needs to be made between those that are undertaken for their own sake and those that are a means to an end. Care should be taken that the project does not become so dominated by activities that there is insufficient opportunity for discussion or flexibility. Discussion should not be based on therapeutic criteria which only the workers understand. This does not mean that discussion should be light-hearted but its purpose should be understood by the adolescents as well as the adults.

Responsibility

Before the project starts the boundaries of responsibility should be clarified. This is vital if one of the major aims of the project is to avoid reception into care. Who takes the final decision about reception into care? Can the project's decision-making procedures actually be implemented? It is relatively easy to agree on responsibility when a crisis is not occurring, but if this agreement fails to be followed in practice it can only serve to undermine the authority of the project staff and the caseworker. A lack of clarity can also confuse and upset the adolescent and his parents.

Family and Community Involvement

Central to the intensive project is the involvement of the family. In one of the projects that we described above the involvement of the family was felt to have been insufficient, although they were involved in establishing the contract and attending review meetings. One solution might be to run parents' groups, or for the project to become responsible for the total social work support offered to the family. These solutions will, of course, require additional staffing for the project.

An issue related to the community is not about its involvement with the project, but relates to the scheme's impact on the community, as the very intensity of the project can create problems. In a community-based project the adolescent may have to return home without having had time to 'wind down' from some of the fairly intense experiences which he has been offered. He may also be returning home to face other challenging and traumatic experiences. It is essential, therefore, that space is created within the programme which assists the process of returning the adolescents relatively 'whole' and able to cope with both the stresses of home and their local community.

The involvement of the community in intermediate treatment is explored further in Chapter 4 as this is a crucial issue in any IT provision and programme, and it distinguishes between the project which is merely located within a community and the project which is community-focused.

4. Mobilizing Community and Neighbourhood Resources

> The community provides the 'natural' basis for our work. Regardless of whether it consists of a cohesive grouping of people with commonly shared traditions, norms, needs and aspirations and with its own structure and indigenous leadership, or whether it is in fact a non-community, an accidental conglomeration of people without any conscious awareness of their common interests, the community's needs and demands, its strengths and weaknesses, potentialities and resources, its traditions and norms, its unity and its conflicts are all significant factors in the growth and development of the community's children. (Leissner, Powley and Evans, 1977)

The above quotation was taken from the report by the National Children's Bureau on their community-based Family Advice Centre/Intermediate Treatment Project. In this chapter we aim to build on the theme of community by considering how the young person's neighbourhood can be taken into account when planning intervention, and how resources within the neighbourhood can be mobilized to assist the adolescent.

But perhaps the first question to ask is how readily do people really accept the immediate local environment as being an important influence on adolescents? As an exercise within several in-service training programmes for social workers and magistrates, the participants were asked to put in order of priority ten factors which it has been suggested might influence and encourage delinquency. Table 4.1 shows the results of this exercise.

This table shows that after the quality of care the adolescent received from his parents, and after the influence of his friends, it was the attitudes of the neighbourhood, and the facilities (or lack of them) within the neighbourhood, that both social workers and magistrates saw as predisposing many adolescents towards delinquency.

Adolescents and parents would seem to agree with the importance of the neighbourhood as an influence on the former (even if they may not attach as much importance to the failings of parental care and supervision in promoting delinquency). As part of a study of perceptions of intermediate treatment (Jones, 1979), parents and adolescents stated that they

Table 4.1   The importance social workers and magistrates attach to some suggested factors which might encourage delinquency

(1 to 10 in decreasing order of importance)

	'Urban' social workers (n = 35)	'Rural' social workers (n = 22)	Justice Court magistrates (n = 65)
Poverty	5	4	5
Peer-group influences	2	2	2
Neighbourhood attitudes	3	6	3
Parental care	1	1	1
Low intelligence	9	8	6
Physical abnormality	10	10	10
Teachers' attitudes	6	5	7
School curriculum	7	7	8
Neighbourhood facilities	4	3	4
Policing policy	8	9	9

NOTE: The most noticeable differences within the rank ordering sequences are:

(a)   The rural social workers were less likely than the urban social workers or the magistrates to see 'neighbourhood attitudes' as being associated with delinquency causation.

(b)   The magistrates tended to stress 'low intelligence' as being associated with delinquency rather more than did the samples of social workers.

These differences would seem to reflect the different environments within which the respondents meet delinquents. For the rural social workers there would not be the same experience of youth street-culture that there was for the urban workers, and for the magistrates it is the adolescents' poor verbal performance in the formal courtroom setting which leads to them seeing delinquents as less intelligent.

saw the aims of intermediate treatment groups as being to keep young people out of trouble. This was to be achieved by keeping them off the streets, relieving their boredom, and compensating for a lack of neighbourhood facilities. As two of the respondents said:

> I spend my time getting into trouble, like going up to the girls' approved school to get chased by the police. There's not much else to do around here which is venturous. The only reason you get into trouble is because it's more venturous (lad, aged 16).

> There's not a lot for kids around here. He spends his time in pubs, trouble, and at the expensive sports centre (mother).

If four groups (social workers, magistrates, parents, and adolescents), who all have a vested interest in intermediate treatment, see the neighbourhood as important, it therefore seems incumbent upon those involved in creating IT provision to make some response. We would argue that there are four main problem areas to tackle.

First, it has already been suggested that some localities may predispose young people towards trouble. This could be due to neighbourhood attitudes (which might not be too concerned with sanctioning delinquent behaviour); through the life-style of the neighbourhood (the culture of the street corner, where children play unsupervised); or simply because of a lack of alternative sources of fun to deflect and divert from delinquency. The task for those involved in providing intermediate treatment could be to press for increased community facilities or an improved use of existing resources, as one method of making the impact of the neighbourhood on the adolescent more positive.

Secondly, it is not just that some neighbourhoods may create difficulties for the adolescent, but that the adolescent may cause problems for the other residents (both older and younger). The tensions that result can often spiral out of all proportion to the incidents which acted as a triggering mechanism, and deteriorating relationships can eventually result in demands on social workers for a particular adolescent to be removed from the community and taken into care. For the great majority of troublesome young people, however, they are more of an annoyance than a danger to the community. Despite this, it may still be important for intermediate treatment to consider it as a part of its task to offer supervision, control, or monitoring in the community to those adolescents who have been a nuisance, or at least to act as an intermediary between the annoying and the annoyed.

Thirdly, and arising out of the above situation, there may be a need to improve the reaction and attitudes of local residents to the adolescent. This can be done by showing the community that those who have been perceived as troublesome and as a nuisance can also have the potential (which is sometimes already realized) to be helpful, constructive, and caring. Again from the National Children's Bureau report, a local councillor comments:

> My own impression is that the best work that has been done from the Family Advice Centres, and with surprising success, has been the use of local youngsters as youth workers. I don't think we should underestimate the value of the work that has been done with these young people, some of whom had a long history of delinquency. (Leissner, Powley and Evans, 1977)

Fourthly, we need to ensure that the programmes we offer to the adolescent outside his neighbourhood (through, for instance, specially created, agency-based IT groups), are relevant to his life within it. There is little point in achieving group or individual goals away from the local community if no change is effected when that individual is returned to it. Conversely, if the adolescent is involved in day care or centre-based projects so intensively that he becomes isolated from his community-based peer group, we need to examine the individual implications when such an intensive involvement ceases.

Having briefly examined these problems, what should the social worker do to help make his intervention more relevant to the adolescent in the context of his neighbourhood? We start below by discussing what could be seen as a major link between the professional and the adolescent: the role of the indigenous volunteer. We focus at some length on the use of volunteers, as this is a key issue in developing a truly *community*-based (rather than an agency-based) service for young people.

Volunteers

One of the major community resources is *people* who are willing to give time and interest to adolescents, especially if they can make a regular commitment over a period of time.

An area intermediate treatment programme, with which one of us was involved, continued for three years, and was based mainly on the commitment of volunteers. The volunteers (a corporal in the army and his wife – a secretary; a corporal in the R.A.F.; a surveyor and his wife – also a secretary; a mature student teacher, whose wife was another secretary; and an apprentice mechanic, who had himself been in care following criminal prosecutions) were recruited in several different ways:

(a)   Self-referral to the agency following a feature article in the local newspaper about the value and usefulness of volunteers.
(b)   Volunteer was already known to the agency as a client.
(c)   Volunteer was 'poached' from the probation service's volunteer group when some probation supervised adolescents were made the subjects of care orders.

The volunteers provided adult supervision for the regular evening and week-end IT programme, were able to obtain many resources not normally available to the social work agency (e.g. rope, maps, marquees from the army; sports equipment from the R.A.F.), and provided expertise and enthusiasm in such things as orienteering, swimming, fishing, and craft work.

However, most valuable of all was the interest and commitment they gave. Altogether over fifty adolescents (boys and girls) were involved in the IT programme, many of them continuing their involvement throughout the three-year period, but it was the time the volunteers gave to the adolescents outside of our structured meetings and events which was probably of greatest significance to the youngsters.

Several of the volunteers lived in the same neighbourhood as the adolescents involved in the programme. The result was that the latter often called on the volunteers for coffee, to take the dog for a walk, to play cards, to sit in the garden and chat, and to help with washing the car. The adolescents would call when they could think of nothing else to do, when they had argued with friends or parents, or just because they preferred the volunteers' company to other options available to them. They sometimes brought their friends with them, so that some volunteers got to know other children in the neighbourhood, including brothers and sisters not included in the IT programme, but who were possibly likely to get into trouble. They did not need to organize any special programme for the adolescents. All that was wanted was a share of the volunteer's attention and personal interest. Obviously this could lead to difficulties as a few of the adolescents were demanding more of the helper's time than they were able to offer. The volunteers had to be helped to say 'no' and to limit their commitment, especially when they or their families were finding the demands personally draining. The volunteers required support in their work with the adolescents (and their families), and this was the social worker's responsibility.

So, what guide-lines need to be considered when working with volunteers? Possibly these could be divided into the three stages of the process of the volunteer's involvement — recruitment, preparation, and support:

Recruitment

Possibly the first hurdle to be overcome is for the social worker to get away from the stereotype of volunteers as lady bountifuls who are eager to distribute their largess and to occupy their time. Volunteers can, and have been, recruited from all sections of the community and from all social classes. Much assistance is already given within many neighbourhoods by friends and neighbours to those in trouble or distress. Hopefully this is something the social worker will aim to support and encourage, possibly by the showing of interest and the offering of praise. Indeed the social worker may be directly in touch with many people who could offer a great deal as befrienders of young people. Parents of adolescent clients can be encouraged to help run groups, clubs, and activities for their children and for other kids in the neighbourhood. Older clients can be linked as befrienders with adolescents who are lacking parental interest or supervision, or who are in conflict with their parents.

The key to the development of a thriving programme is to be innovative and imaginative in one's search for potential help. This might include making use of the obvious avenues of advertising – such as the Press, local radio, talks to community groups, and leafleting. But in the end it is likely to be those with whom you are able to establish *personal* contact who are most likely to be responsive to the suggestion that they have something to offer young people. They might be clients on your caseload, neighbours of the young people (including people like shopkeepers and local police-men), friends with whom *you* share your leisure, and other professionals with whom you come into contact (teachers and health visitors would seem to have particular relevance). The development of a patch system obviously makes it easier to become aware of, and to approach, local people who might be willing and able to help. As the Aves Report on *The Voluntary Worker in the Social Services* (1969) states: 'It seems to us that it is attitude rather than background which is important, and the main object of extending the field of recruitment is to obtain more volun-teers with understanding, sensitivity and the will to help.'

Preparation

Following the process of recruiting potential volunteers, is the problem of selecting out those who would seem to be unsuitable. To a large extent this should be accomplished by the unsuitable volunteers themselves if the preparation process is adequate. Preparation should include stressing the need for a *continuing* commitment from the volunteers towards the adolescents, and a willingness to endure testing-out and rejection by them. When confronted with these issues some volunteers may decide to withdraw. It is much better that they do so at this stage rather than raising the interests and hopes of adolescents which they then fail to attempt to sustain or meet.

However, preparation should also include highlighting for the volunteers what they have to offer the adolescents. They do not need to be expert mountain climbers or skilled model-makers to be able to *share* and stimu-late the interests of the adolescents and to show that they care. It is commitment and personal involvement that most of the adolescents seek. As we suggested in the previous chapter, activities are the means that allow the demonstration of caring and sharing, rather than being an end in themselves. However, many volunteers will have interests which they can readily offer to adolescents (gardening, football supporting, swim-ming, fishing, car maintenance, etc.) but these may need highlighting so that they can be used as useful vehicles for establishing relationships.

The key issue in preparation still remains the *realistic* examination of commitment. Setting limits as to what is a tolerable level of involvement can often be as much a problem for the social worker as for the volunteer, but this becomes even more pertinent when worker and client live in close proximity to one another. Not only do personal involvement thresholds need to be taken into account, but so also do those of your family and friends. It is difficult to be responsive and caring if:

(a)   your spouse becomes obsessed about the silver being pinched,
(b)   your children become jealous of the amount of attention that other kids are getting,
(c)   your neighbours pointedly rush indoors the minute you and your adolescent gang emerge.

Such problems are common enough to the residential worker who lives 'on site' and it would seem pointless, apart from being personally damaging, to extend such difficulties into the community. However, for many volunteers and their families (as for residential workers), close involvement with adolescents can be rewarding, satisfying, and enjoyable; it is therefore just as important to stress the potential benefits as much as the disadvantages.

Support

Throughout contact with the adolescents the volunteer has the right to support from the social worker, although at present many volunteers would appear not to receive this. A recent study commissioned by the British Association of Social Workers, commented that:

> Just over one-half of local authority social workers and seven-tenths of probation officers are working with volunteers. The most typical relationship between social workers and volunteers in the local authority services is one where the volunteers do not work under the direct guidance of the social worker, and where there is little, if any, personal contact between them. In the probation service, the most typical relationship is a direct one characterised by close and personal contact. (Holme and Maizels, 1978)

This finding of Holme and Maizels reflects the different functions that volunteers might have in the context of social service departments (e.g. delivering meals-on-wheels) compared particularly with the now established use of voluntary associates as befrienders in the probation service. However, it may need stressing that volunteers who are working with our adolescent clients need to be regularly supported and supervised – as Barr found in his research on the use of volunteers in the probation service:

> Almost all voluntary associates welcomed regular support and consultation. Occasionally a voluntary associate tended to become overdependent or alternatively might fail to consult the probation officer for fear of being a nuisance or because he was thought to be too busy, but most recognised, in a mature way, their dependence upon the skill and experience of the probation officer. (Barr, 1971)

Support and supervision should offer the volunteer an opportunity to discuss the continuing development of his work with the adolescents. There are many issues that may be raised. Seeing the social worker as an expert is likely to create demands for understanding as to why the adolescent acts in particular ways. How do you deal with behaviour that challenges or confronts? How do you help someone who you know has problems but refuses to discuss them? The social worker's task extends not only to offering answers, but also to providing positive reassurance or constructive criticism. In addition to this, there is a need to monitor the work being undertaken, so that appropriate responses can be offered.

So, how is this support and supervision to be offered? What does it require from the social worker? First of all it requires *time*, and agencies should not see the use of volunteer befrienders as necessarily being a way of saving social worker time. It takes time to recruit, select, support, and supervise volunteers. The gain is that the service that the adolescent ultimately receives is likely to be greatly enriched by the commitment and enthusiasm of the volunteer.

Secondly, it requires an awareness on the part of the social worker of what it is like to be a volunteer. The volunteer may be isolated from others who are also befriending adolescents, and have had no prior experience of consciously setting-out to get to know adolescents who they may not have met before (this, of course, is less likely to apply if the volunteers live within the same neighbourhood as the adolescents).

Thirdly, it is important that the volunteer is not seen as some type of second-class social worker. Rather, the volunteer is someone who has much to offer the adolescent in his own right. The social worker who patronizes volunteers, and who attempts to maintain a status differential and social distance between himself and the volunteer, suggests that he is not aware of the real potential volunteers have to befriend adolescents. The patronizing social worker is also unlikely to receive the respect and confidence of the volunteer. Working with volunteers should be based on partnership, not patronization, although it must be remembered that the social worker ultimately remains responsible for the over-all service that the adolescent receives.

Fourthly, the social worker must be willing to accept confrontation from the volunteer. Many volunteers quite rightly come to question the standard of social work service that their adolescents receive. They may well become a leading advocate for the adolescents that they get to know. They may, for example, petition for additional financial assistance for the adolescent's family. Sometimes the demands they make on behalf of the adolescents may be inappropriate, exaggerated, and based on a lack of information about some aspect of the adolescent's life. Conversely, the demands the volunteers may make are often likely to be very appropriate, and will reflect a growing commitment of the volunteer to the adolescent, and a growing awareness of the failings of social workers and their agencies.

Lastly, the social work agency needs to ensure that the volunteer is:

(a) adequately covered by insurance. . . . This should include personal cover for the volunteer, for those for whom he becomes responsible through his voluntary work, and for the volunteer's property (e.g. his car, if he uses this in his work with the adolescents),

(b) adequately recompensed for any expenses he incurs (e.g. milage payments),

(c) receiving adequate support. In particular, it is important that the volunteer knows how to contact the social worker if a crisis should occur with the adolescents with whom he is working,

(d) recognized formally by the agency as an associate worker, so that the volunteer is offered some identity with regard to the agency.

The mobilization of people as a community resource can therefore be crucial, whether the intermediate treatment scheme is community- or centre-based. The following description, from the report of Hammersmith Teenage Project, helps to illustrate this:

> The project has nevertheless demonstrated that a variety of 'community links' can be mobilised to support and exert a positive influence on a teenager at risk. In forming any such links, the aim is to locate people with whom the teenager relates well and whom he respects, who can exercise a stabilising and positive influence on him. An additional aim in many cases will be to put the teenager in situations where he can develop his talents positively and constructively and gain a sense of personal achievement.
>
> The project found that the first type of 'community link' which can be developed is support from relatives, close friends of the family and 'proxy parents, aunts or uncles'. Even in the large impersonal blocks of flats . . . there is some evidence to suggest that people on the same floor can be found who are prepared to give a teenager support.
>
> The second type of 'community link' is that which goes further than merely forming a one-to-one link and involves the teenager in the local community's activities in some way — for example, as play leader in a summer play scheme for younger children organised

by or with a local tenants' association, or by other forms of community service. . . .

The third type of community link can be provided by work experience programmes, where local employers agree to take a teenager for a couple of days a week. (National Association for the Care and Resettlement of Offenders (NACRO), 1978)

Organized Amenities

People, however, are only one form of neighbourhood resource. There are many others, such as existing youth provision, clubs and societies, and even the use of empty property. In attempting to develop intermediate treatment, the social worker should attempt to tackle two issues; one is a greater use of existing facilities, and the second is a reduction in alienation that the adolescent may well feel towards clubs and organizations that he has already rejected, or who have rejected him.

It may be appropriate for the intermediate treatment programme to be based in a local club or hall, where the adolescent experiences a programme geared to his needs but in a setting which he had previously perceived as a non-viable option for himself. There may then be long-term gains if the adolescent continues to use the facility outside the IT programme. This, however, also requires that if the adolescent is to continue to use these neighbourhood facilities, they must also be available to him outside of the IT programme.

Our own experience is rather mixed. In some areas we have found local youth clubs and schools accepting of those involved in intermediate treatment. Youth workers, teachers, and the police have shared in activities with the groups, allowing premises to be used and, where appropriate, encouraging continuing involvement by the adolescents. In other areas youth workers have appeared more concerned about safeguarding the fabric of their clubs (and of their existing membership) instead of trying to provide a service for young people involved in intermediate treatment. The reasons and rationale behind such moves can be various; sometimes those involved in intermediate treatment have already been ejected from those clubs, and sometimes the leader is concerned with only highly organized and structured activities. Occasionally the pressure comes from the management committee, who do not wish to pursue what they see as a risk to *their* premises. Whatever the reason, it is still important for the worker to attempt negotiation, as even the worst outcome can be no change, whereas the best could be a considerable improvement.

The youth club and youth workers are only one of the areas that the social worker could begin to examine. Schools are clearly another area. Some intermediate treatment schemes, such as the Hammersmith Teenage

Project and Islington Family Service Unit, provide day care/educational facilities, but even where that is not done, or such a project is felt too ambitious, there are still other roles to be performed. Encouraging more out-of-school hours activities, and promoting inter-agency projects, are possibilities. Schools are the one resource that can be found in most neighbourhoods, and therefore they can become the ideal venue for a variety of community services.

Two problems, however, often seem to stand in the way of such development. One is that inter-professional competition can often become a pseudonym for buck-passing, the argument being that 'it's not really our responsibility but somebody else's'. It is necessary to cross professional boundaries to create new forms of community provision. However, where an adolescent is on a supervision order, and particularly where there is a risk of that individual being received into residential care, then the major onus for initiating action would clearly seem to rest with the social worker.

Why, for instance, do social workers so frequently fail to respond to young people saying that they are bored? One answer could be that they see leisure provision as the responsibility of the youth service. Another explanation could be that during their own adolescence, which for the majority was blessed with a greater degree of academic success, it was a relatively unusual phenomenon. As we have argued before, intermediate treatment is not all backpacks and mountain climbing. Although an individual social worker may feel relatively powerless, he or she still carries far more influence and 'clout' than any adolescent in the community. Therefore taking on the role of advocate or negotiator in creating improved amenities and facilities can be just as valuable as any other role for the social worker.

Physical Environment

In many areas the physical environment may be seen as more of a problem than a resource, but the use within intermediate treatment of open spaces for activities, and the exploration of the physical environment as an activity in its own right, may be appropriate ways of helping our adolescents feel more at home in their neighbourhood. One IT group compiled an index of local shops, comparing the range of goods sold in each one. They divided into small sub-groups, with an adult attached to each group, and divided their shopping centre into patches. Each sub-group then surveyed the shops within their patch. They wrote down what each shop sold (some groups initially tape-recorded this information and then transcribed it), and then met together to compile one report. This was then typed, and one lad designed a cartoon cover for the report. The index included over sixty shops, and copies were left at the health centre, the police station, and the library as a take-away information source for local people.

Another exercise was to get adolescents to take photographs of their neighbourhood, and then to use these photographs to stimulate a discussion about what it is like to live in the area. This also allows the social worker to get some idea of how the adolescent uses the neighbourhood . . . where he meets his friends, where he plays, and where he is likely to get into trouble.

Some intermediate treatment groups as a part of their programme organize visits to *local services* – such as the post office, fire station, or police station (which may not be unknown already to a few of our clients!), with the intention of helping the adolescents to understand what services are available locally and how they work. Visits to local industries might serve the same purpose of presenting aspects of the local environment which may normally be 'out of bounds' to young people as living and functional parts of community life.

But probably the most influential type of neighbourhood resource for the adolescents is likely to be the street-corner *natural friendship group*. Many of us will have had experience of young people coming to the office for their interview accompanied by their friends, who then hang about in the car park, in the doorway, ride up and down in the lift, or annoy the receptionist in the reception area-cum-waiting-room. It might be appropriate for us to consider moving outside of the realm of our defined 'client' to work with these naturally existing friendship groups, as these are the groups which may be of greater significance to our clients than specially created, formal IT groups which are initially composed of strangers.

Indeed, the emphasis throughout this chapter is that intermediate treatment is more likely to be relevant to the adolescents if it is integrated into their lives within their neighbourhood. In the long term not only may this make IT more meaningful and helpful for the adolescents, but it is also likely to make it more acceptable to them, as it takes into account their understanding of why kids get into trouble. Trouble for them is associated with boredom, lack of neighbourhood facilities, and pressure from peers out on the street-corner. By relating intermediate treatment to the neighbourhood in which the adolescent lives, some of these issues can be tackled.

5. Evaluation, Training and Staff Support

In the last three chapters we have looked at some of the elements that practitioners might include in programmes of intermediate treatment. In this, and Chapter 6, we look at some of the issues and concerns that might help or hinder social workers when implementing programmes of IT. We start by examining the evaluation of intermediate treatment, how it can be undertaken, and used.

Evaluation

The evaluation of intermediate treatment has four potential purposes. It can help to influence policy and therefore have a political function; it may help to involve the consumers more fully in the services that they receive; it can help to improve programme planning and content; and it can be used in furthering staff development.

Influencing Policy

One argument for research and evaluation of intermediate treatment is that if IT can be seen to work and to achieve its goals then this will assist the argument that intermediate treatment should be further resourced. There are two reservations with regard to this argument. First, it is difficult to measure the effectiveness of any form of social intervention in terms of its outcome, especially if its aim is to influence behaviour and this is how outcome is to be assessed. The difficulty is in controlling all the variables, all the influences, which impinge on any individual. An intermediate treatment programme may have a lot of positive influence on a young offender, but he may still continue to offend in response to overriding pressure from his peers or as a result of frustration and anger created by conflict within his home. We may be able to assess the positive impact that involvement in intermediate treatment has on the adolescent by 'before and after' measures of his self-concept or his self-esteem, but there is no guarantee that improved self-esteem will necessarily reduce his offending, and this leaves us with the dilemma identified by Allard:

> Put crudely, neither the courts nor society is impressed by the fact that an apathetic, unhealthy, isolated, inadequate and culturally deprived delinquent has become, as a result of intensive social work intervention, an imaginative, athletic, companionable, adequate and culturally enriched delinquent. (Allard, 1976)

The second reservation is that even if intermediate treatment can be shown to reduce the incidence of (re)offending by adolescents, there is no guarantee that those who formulate social policy, or who sentence juveniles in the courts, will be influenced by this success. As Millham has noted:

> I would stress to you that the residential tradition is very strong. It has been going for nearly 300 years and it is not going to be shifted by a few murmurs about intermediate treatment, particularly when children are often popped in institutions by an administrative elite who have been educated in similar places and whose ideas of adolescent heaven is a whiff of Lifebuoy soap and sweaty socks.
>
> Nor will it disappear just because you can demonstrate the abilities of IT. In the old approved school system demonstrations that the failure rates were enormous or that the institutions had a host of other difficulties were irrelevant for policy, simply because residential institutions have one enormous advantage over community care. Behind their walls the children are not visible, and if they run away and cause trouble, they are obviously extremely difficult – a view which justifies institutional practice. In contrast, if an offender placed on a community project misbehaves, people see this as your fault. Far from justifying your position, the problems which the adolescent poses reproach the intervention. (Millham, 1977)

As we have shown in Chapter 1 we do not just associate intermediate treatment with delinquency prevention. We also see a major role for IT in countering the deprivation which some adolescents experience, regardless of whether this deprivation is associated with delinquency. However, we also noted in Chapter 1 that social values have changed since the 1960s, and that intermediate treatment is only likely to receive any substantial increase in resources if it is seen to tackle delinquency more effectively, and more cheaply, than residential and custodial placements. In one sense this should not be too difficult when it costs £200 a week to keep a juvenile in a community home with education, £30,000 capital expenditure and £400 recurring weekly expenditure to provide one secure placement, and when three-quarters of these youngsters then reoffend when returned to the community! However, while the intensity of IT programmes remains low, the influences on the adolescent which encourage his offending are many and intense, and social attitudes still see the young petty offender as an outcast to be isolated from the community, then the task of arguing the effectiveness of intermediate treatment, and of getting resources reallocated to this form of social provision, is far from easy.

There still remains, however, a responsibility to look at the effectiveness of intermediate treatment, and any outcome research should consider the following issues:

(a)   What were the goals of the IT programme?

(b)   Are the measuring instruments being used within the research appropriate to measure whether the goals have been attained?

(c)   Was any change which occurred between the beginning and end of the programme a result of the programme's impact or was it due to chance or the influence of other variables? To answer this question satisfactorily requires the establishment of control groups (based on matched samples or random allocation), and large enough samples to allow for statistical analysis. However, in the absence of a large, controlled experiment, the adolescents involved in the programme could be used (less satisfactorily) as their own control by comparing their 'before' and 'after' scores on the measuring instrument.

Consumer Involvement

A problem with much social intervention is that it takes away or reduces the control the client has over his life. Decisions are made and plans implemented which affect the client, but over which he has no control. He is often not even involved in the planning or decision-making process. By getting consumers to comment on the services that they receive, and by considering and acting upon these comments when planning future programmes, we achieve two goals. First, we increase the client's involvement in what is being planned, and, secondly, we are likely to plan an improved service by listening to the clients' views.

Clients' views can be obtained by questionnaires and interviews (see, for instance, Jones, 1979), but they can also be obtained through group discussion. The following comments were made when the adolescents in one IT group were asked about their views of the group:

Ray: 'What's the point of this group?'

Chris: 'We get to do things we wouldn't normally do.'

Wendy: 'That's only a part of it though, isn't it?'

Andy: 'It helps to guide us on the right lines.'

Wendy: 'I can't see how.'

Andy: 'Well, we're talking about things more; more than we would at home, and thinking things ourselves instead of having another adult thinking for us. Down here we talk more about the things we should be doing instead of what we shouldn't be doing, and we're talking about reasoning with each other instead of going to parents all the time.'

The consumer's evaluation of the intervention he receives is always of importance. It gives some information about the appropriateness of the intervention for that client, and offers hints as to how other clients are likely to respond to this form of service. It can also highlight points of conflict between the perspectives of the service providers (e.g. the social workers) and the recipients of the service, and these possible conflicts can then be considered in planning future programmes.

Improving Programmes

A major aim of evaluation should be to improve the service offered to clients. This requires that evaluation includes looking at what the service contains, how it is offered, and its results. Much of this evaluation can be undertaken by practitioners, such as monitoring the changing patterns of relationship within a group. This might be useful when attempting to influence those patterns, perhaps by attempting to integrate isolates into the group, or when challenging delinquent cliques. Fig. 5.1 gives an example of a sociogram, which is one way of looking at relationship patterns.

Fig. 5.1

An example of a sociogram

	strong relationship	———————
KEY	weak relationship	– – – – –
	direction of relationship	——————▶

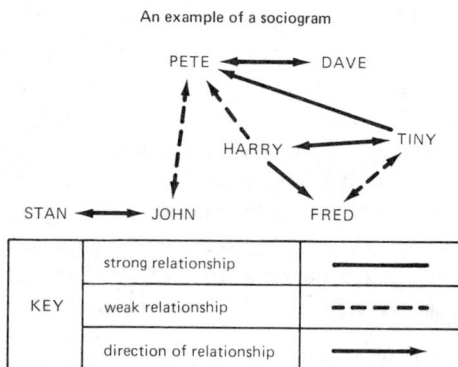

In using sociograms:

(a)   It may be that they tell you nothing new about the group. Even if this is so, they help one to focus on relationships within the group in post-group discussions.

(b)   They can indicate potential problems ahead. For example, in Fig. 5.1 if John is absent from the group then Stan is likely to be isolated, and

if Tiny is absent then all Harry's relationships are initiated by him and may not be reciprocated.

(c) They can show strengths and weaknesses within the group. In the figure Pete seems to be the leader in the group as shown by the number of people who seek contact with him.

(d) If one of the aims of the group is to increase the awareness of the group's members, it may be appropriate to feed back to them the information depicted in sociograms.

We have used several techniques in addition to sociograms, in order to monitor what is happening within adolescent groups:

(i) checklists (completed by leaders after each meeting):

Checklists should be adjusted so that the questions asked are relevant to the purpose of the group. For example, if the group is about reducing aggression and aggressive feelings, then you would want to compile checklists that included behaviour categories such as aggressive, dominant, passive, clam, etc.

Fig. 5.2

Member Number

	1	2	3	4
aggressive				
dominant		✓	✓	
passive				
calm	✓			
active	✓			
subdued				

(ii) questionnaires:

Who makes most noise in the group?
Who makes good suggestions?
Who does most of the work?

This information can then be displayed on a chart and used to stimulate group discussion. Try and ensure that something *positive* is said about everyone, even if you have to create a question aimed at only one individual, such as:

Who tells the best jokes?
Who put the lock on our trunk?

(iii) sentence completions:

The best thing about this group is . . .
When I come to the group I feel . . .
The worse thing about this group is . . .
People in the group sometimes make me feel . . .

Again this information can often usefully be fed back to the adolescents.

(iv) attitude scales:

people in the group are:

      KIND__ __ __ __ __ __ __UNKIND
      NOISY__ __ __ __ __ __ __QUIET
      FUN__ __ __ __ __ __ __ BORING

By using these techniques at different times during the programme, changes in perception can be monitored and current issues in the group identified. These can then be discussed with the adolescents as well as helping the social workers to plan their continuing work with the group. Similar techniques can also be used with individuals not involved in groups when attempting to get them to comment on the service they are receiving, or when exploring with them current issues in their lives.

Staff Development

Evaluation techniques, such as those described above, can be used in helping staff to improve their performance and their skills. For instance, it can help social workers to heighten their awareness of what is happening within a group. This process can also include improving the adults' awareness of themselves, and their impact on others, if questions on them are included in the sentence completion tests or the attitude scales, and if the adults also plot themselves on the sociogram. For this information to be used constructively, it is helpful to have the assistance of a consultant who can help the adults to face and clarify some of the personal and professional issues that involvement in intermediate treatment will raise. This increase in awareness of ourselves and of others should form part of basic training as well as being a focus for continuing staff development.

Training for Intermediate Treatment

At many of the courses and conferences that have been focused on inter-mediate treatment over the last few years there has often been the tendency for people to talk about intermediate treatment as if it is a particular method, such as task-centred casework or family therapy. We would disagree with this assumption and would argue that: *(a)* IT is not a method, but a generic term for a range of skills and services directed towards young people and their families; *(b)* the more specialist IT becomes, then the further away it is likely to get from acting as a catalyst for integrating services that are too separated, such as family counselling and peer-group work; *(c)* IT needs to maintain strong links with the mainstream of social work so that in developing new work strategies the benefits gained can be felt by other areas of practice, for example in services for the elderly and the mentally ill.

Therefore any training course focused on intermediate treatment needs to cover a wide range of topics and should include:

(a) Aiding understanding and awareness of adolescents and adolescence. What is it like to be 14, female and going out on your first date? What are the major concerns and worries of 16-year-old school leavers?
(b) Developing skills and techniques that improve our interaction with young people.
(c) Challenging our traditional assumptions about how to work. Are interviews in the office the best way to structure our contact? Is it always appropriate to be thinking that the solution to any adolescent difficulty is groupwork?
(d) Considering those organizational skills and political strategies which are necessary to influence agency management, and also the attitudes of other agencies and organizations (including courts).

Table 5.1 depicts a potential short training programme (based on a course which we provided for a local social services department) for a five-day course on 'Working with Adolescents'. This course was planned as an attempt to stimulate practitioners to look at their work with young people and to improve some of their basic skills. We included material on the experience of being adolescent, on direct work with young people, their families and communities, and also examined working within, and on, the organizational and political arena which affects policy. The course included a good deal of experiential learning, as we felt this was likely to give the participants confidence to try different techniques, and to use alternative perspectives in their everyday work.

Table 5.1   *An in-service training programme on 'Working with Adolescents'*

INTRODUCTION	Small groups on the memories/recollections of the feelings of our adolescence	
GETTING IN TOUCH WITH ADOLESCENCE	Film: *Summer of '42* and discussion	Social development during adolescence: a review of the research
Disturbance and breakdown during adolescence: lecture/discussion	Structuring an interview with an adolescent: one model using role repertory grid technique	Alternative strategies for working with adolescents: two simulation exercises (see below)
FAMILY CONFLICT		
Role plays and discussion on adolescent/parent conflict and social worker intervention	Film: *Family Life* and discussion	CONSIDERING RESIDENTIAL CARE The role of residential placement. The process of reception into care (using *Signs of Trouble* series recordings)
GROUPWORK WITH ADOLESCENTS		
Structuring and forming groups: (discussion based on checklist in Chapter 2)	Using processes within the group: discussing and describing the response to an incident of theft within a group	
THE ADOLESCENT IN THE COMMUNITY		
Working within a neighbourhood, with volunteers and other agencies: a discussion of the work of one project	Simulation game based on decision-making about difficult adolescents in a community	COURSE FEEDBACK

The programme described in Table 5.1 is no more than an introduction to some of the skills and perspectives needed in intermediate treatment. It also needs to be supported by more focused courses (for example, on groupwork, and working with volunteers), to be followed by the worker receiving related supervision and consultation as he develops some of these approaches within his own practice, and to be integrated with courses specifically aimed at managers and policy-makers.

Alternative Strategies for Working with Adolescents – 2 Exercises

One of the issues looked at within the training course was the difficulty of broadening perspectives when considering how to intervene in the life of an adolescent. Two complementary exercises were designed to do this:

Exercise 1: Exploring Adolescent Problems (a lateral thinking/brain-storming exercise)

Goal:

To encourage participants to explore the range of adolescent problems, based on their own experience, and to look at some potential solutions to these problems; to allow all people in the group to make some contribution; to compare lateral and vertical thinking systems (see also p. 108).

Group Size:

Any number between twelve and twenty-four participants. Longer time will be needed as the number of participants increases. Three work groups should be created, with an equal number in each. While not working on this exercise, groups may be completing another exercise (for example, Exercise 2 below) which does not require the continuous services of the instructor. The other exercise should be one that uses an alternative thinking process to this exercise, which aims to explore a wide variety of options rather than examine one specific option in depth.

Time Required:

Approximately two hours (two and a half hours if combined with Exercise 2).

Materials:

A felt marker for every third participant.
A roll of masking tape.
At least twelve 10 cm x 5 cm plain index cards for each participant.

Physical Setting:

A room with enough space for all the participants to meet to discuss the exercise. Two additional rooms for the two work groups who at any one time will not be directly involved in this exercise. A large area of blank wall or board.

Process:

(a)   Starting with *Work Group A*, each participant receives a felt marker and approximately ten cards. They are asked to write on each card one problem that they think adolescents frequently experience. It should be stressed that they only write one problem per card, that they write in such a way that the card can easily be read, and that if they run out of cards more cards are available.

(b)   After about ten minutes the cards are collected, shuffled, and then taped to the wall. At this stage it does not matter in which order they are placed.

(c)   The participants in Group A are now asked to look at the sum total of their work, and asked if they can see any problems which can be grouped together. After removing duplicate cards, and rewriting unclear cards, about five to ten problem clusters usually remain.

(d)   Finally, Group A is asked if there are any problem areas missing, and if so, cards can be written to cover these areas.

(e)   *Work Group B* now starts its part of the exercise by looking at the problem areas highlighted by Group A. Depending on the number of problem clusters identified by Group A, a cluster is then assigned to either individuals or small syndicates in Group B. Each of these individuals or syndicates then receives a stack of cards and is asked to write on each one possible solutions to the problems noted in their problem cluster.

(f)   These are then displayed on the wall next to the problem cluster to which they relate, and Group B is then given the opportunity to add any problem solutions which it thinks are missing.

(g)   *Work Group C* then repeats the same exercise, only this time looking for blockages to the potential solutions.

(h)   At the end of the exercise the three work groups join together for a discussion of the work that they have produced, and they are asked to look at the relevance of the ideas displayed for *their* social work practice and planning.

Variations:

(a)   At the beginning or end of the exercise a short lecture could be given on the use of brainstorming and lateral thinking, as similar exercises might be used directly with adolescents, when, for instance, involving them in activity planning.

(b) A fourth stage could be added to the exercise to look at ways of overcoming the blockages identified by Work Group C.

(c) The participants could be asked to look at the dynamics of groups involved in this type of exercise, as opposed to different work methods.

In the exercise described above, only one of the work groups would be involved in the exercise at any one time. When the work groups are not involved in Exercise 1 they could be asked to complete Exercise 2, which is described below. Therefore, the programme for this training session would be:

	Group A	Group B	Group C
20 minutes	Introduction to both exercises		
20 minutes	Exercise 1	Exercise 2	Exercise 2
20 minutes	Exercise 2	Exercise 1	Exercise 2
20 minutes	Exercise 2	Exercise 1	Exercise 2
25 minutes	Discussion of issues identified in Exercise 1.		
45 minutes	Presentation by *each* group of their proposals in response to Exercise 2.		

Exercise 2: Alternative Project Proposals in Working with Adolescents (a planning exercise)

Goal:

To enable participants to practise project planning.
To rehearse preparation and presentation of project plans to management.

Scenario:

Your department has made available to your team (your work group) some extra resources. You have available £12,000 and a small disused church hall. You are asked to present to the management team, who in turn will need to present your proposals to the social services committee, *three* proposals for the use of the money and premises in developing a social work project to benefit adolescents.

You will need to:

(a) consider the objectives to be achieved by the projects you propose, what you would need to offer to achieve the objectives, and to cost your programme (i.e. itemize anticipated expenditure),

(b) discuss the advantages and disadvantages of each project proposal,

(c) place the three proposals into a priority ranking.

Your team will be required to submit and discuss your proposals with the other course members as though they are the management team.

It is suggested that you use large sheets of paper and the felt markers to allow you to present your proposals visually as charts, diagrams, lists, etc.

Time Required:

Approximately 1 hour and 45 minutes (see timetable above).

Materials:

At least one felt marker for each work group, several large sheets of paper (the reverse side of rolls of wallpaper would be suitable), and masking tape to allow the paper to be hung on the walls.

Physical Setting:

A room in which each group can meet, including at least one room which is large enough for the plenary sessions at the beginning and end of the exercise. This room should have wall space to allow each group to display their proposals.

Variations:

There is scope to vary the extent to which the presentation of the project proposals is role played. For instance, you may wish to structure a small group to role play the management team or social services committee, with other course members observing and commenting on the role play.

Extending Training

We have focused above on the provision of in-service training as, in the short term, this seems the best way to meet the needs of a large number of workers in an agency or area, and hopefully they will then be able to mutually support and encourage each other. Together they may also have more impact on the perspectives and organization of their agencies.

To achieve most effect, this type of course needs to be able to build on strong foundations laid during initial training, but, as yet, few basic qualifying courses offer a particular focus on work with adolescents in the community. In-service training should also be built upon by full-time, post-qualifying studies.

In the absence of full-time training resources, workers should consider their own potential to provide support and stimulation for one another. In this context the skills and experience of youth workers and teachers should not be ignored. There is great scope for joint inter-professional training programmes not only to improve our own work, but also to have an impact on the perspectives and work of other agencies. Through greater co-operation in joint ventures mutual understanding can be increased and a more comprehensive service offered to those adolescents who are the common concern of many workers and agencies.

Staff Support

Diversity is both one of the attractions and one of the problems of intermediate treatment, and this is reflected in our discussion below on offering support to intermediate treatment workers. In Chapter 2 we advocated the use of consultants when running IT groups, but as intermediate treatment is not just about groupwork, the issue of staff support becomes wider than that of obtaining groupwork consultancy.

Support is required both for the generic social worker involved in intermediate treatment, and for the full-time specialist IT worker. For the generic worker there are four areas in which he should be offered support: those of time, finance, recognition, and team commitment, each of which have the potential to be contentious issues.

A common grumble from social workers involved in intermediate treatment is that 'management supports us providing it doesn't cost anything and that we do it in our own time'. Intermediate treatment may be a cheaper option than residential provision but it still calls for a financial and manpower commitment. This might include offering social workers financial payment for the additional hours worked, or allowing and encouraging them to take time in lieu. If time in lieu is offered, then to make it realistic requires some reduction in other areas of the social worker's work-load. If payments or time in lieu are not offered to the social worker then three reactions are likely to occur:

(a) Social workers do not involve themselves in intermediate treatment, although they consider that this involvement would be preferable to their present work-styles. They therefore feel an increasing degree of job dissatisfaction.

(b) They are also likely to feel an increasing degree of job dissatisfaction if they involve themselves in intermediate treatment programmes in their own time with no rewards or recognition from their agency. This is likely to lead to an increase in their over-all level of stress and to increasing work frustration (see, for example, Herzberg, 1968). This results in high staff turnover, which disrupts the work being undertaken. One study of intermediate treatment showed that a third of the adolescents involved in IT groups had a change of caseworker within a year (Jones, 1978).

(c) The quality of the service offered to the clients deteriorates. There is disruption as a result of staff changes, and the over-all service remains

underdeveloped as other staff become reluctant to increase their involvement in what is seen as an 'optional' area of work.

Support for those involved in intermediate treatment does not just include offering time and money. It also includes showing recognition of the value of the work being undertaken. As one social worker commented to us:

> It's not just running groups in our own time, but a feeling that it's worth while and appreciated by management.When we came back from our residential week I passed the area officer in the corridor. He never spoke, although he knew all about the group. If only he had said 'How did it go?' or 'Did everything work out all right?', it would make you feel that they cared about what you were doing. That's much more important.

Recognition needs to come from immediate colleagues as well as from social work managers. How many social workers, having been on a residential experience for the first time, return to the office to be met with comments such as 'Did you enjoy your holiday?' Joking, but unthinking, comments like this are much more harmful than helpful.

Team support, therefore, is especially important for the social worker who is involved in the emotionally and often physically demanding tasks of intermediate treatment. Cynical and hurtful comments are most often made to those involved in IT when this involvement reflects a personal rather than a team commitment. Without wishing to be over-analytical, team members not involved in intermediate treatment may well feel, if not jealous, perhaps left out when they see their colleagues gaining satisfaction from intermediate treatment. These feelings are likely to be increased by having to cover office duty, or crises in the IT worker's caseload, when the worker is away with the adolescents. Intermediate treatment needs to have the support and commitment of all the workers in the team if it is to flourish.

All the points which we have raised so far apply to the generic, team-based social worker and to the specialist, area-based IT worker. In Chapter 6 we look in more detail at the positioning of specialist intermediate treatment posts within social services departments, but in the context of staff support the specialist worker has particular problems which are caused by him having lateral functions within a vertical system of accountability. These lateral functions mean that the specialist worker crosses many boundaries, such as the methods of casework, groupwork, and community work; the client boundaries of children, families, and possibly mental and physical handicap; and the setting boundaries of field, day, and residential care. A problem for the intermediate treatment specialist is how to gain appropriate support and supervision. It is therefore of little surprise that many specialist workers speak of the isolation of their job and the difficulties that this causes for them.

Three crucial issues for the specialist worker are supervision, accountability, and involvement. Supervision and accountability are linked issues, for supervision (as compared to consultancy) includes a management function, and management includes a process of accountability. Supervision of workers involved in intermediate treatment is difficult because it is unlikely that any one supervisor will have knowledge about, or experience of, the many and varied tasks which might come under the umbrella of 'intermediate treatment', including, for instance, groupwork, community work, family counselling, working with volunteers, and inter-agency liaison. But for the social worker the supervisor is a central and important figure:

> The key figure in staff development programmes is the immediate staff supervisor of the worker. Evidence is now accumulating at every level on the importance of the first line manager. He is the one with the immediate responsibility for the context in which the worker finds himself, and staff development relates also to the context as well as extending the individual worker. (Warwick, 1977)

As the contexts covered by intermediate treatment are so broad, it is often essential that supervision is supplemented by specialist consultancy, but the support and encouragement offered by the supervisor remain of great importance.

But who should offer the supervision? To whom should the IT specialist be accountable? In many authorities one gains the impression that accountability for new posts becomes a balancing act between the competing demands and aspirations of different sections within the organization. It is of crucial importance that the specialist practitioner is located within the organization in such a way that he is involved in decision-making and case planning with regard to *all* adolescent clients, and that his accountability reflects this location. His supervisor, therefore, should be someone who also has over-all responsibility for decision-making about adolescent clients and about social workers' work-loads. This might be a team leader, area officer, or it may be a principal officer who has responsibility for services to children.

If intermediate treatment is really to have an impact within agencies, and if it is to influence the way in which the agency handles its work, then specialist workers need to be centrally involved in decision-making about services for adolescents. For the practitioner, it is important that he is not shunted into some organizational siding where the day-by-day work of the agency rushes by with occasionally a case or two pointed in his direction by a social worker who has decided that 'this is a suitable case for IT'. Intermediate treatment specialist practitioners need to be included within the mainstream of social work and should, for instance, be involved in whatever review system the agency operates with regard to the adolescents who are its responsibility.

Consultancy

Many of the skills and approaches involved in intermediate treatment remain relatively underdeveloped in most social work agencies. These include those areas we have already discussed, such as recruiting and supporting volunteers, and working with groups. It is often necessary for advice to be sought when workers are exploring new approaches within an agency and while this advice may be available within the organization, it may often have to be obtained from external consultants.

It is our belief, for example, that all groups run by social workers should have (and use) access to one constant individual who is outside the group but who can help the social workers to explore and reflect on their work. The groupworkers and the consultant should meet regularly, thereby enabling discussion of conflicts which may arise over worker-style and leadership. It should also help the workers to identify previously unrecognized processes and issues within the group by giving time and space for thought and reflection.

The Lippitts (1977) identify eight roles which might be performed by a consultant and Fig. 5.3 locates these roles on their directive/non-directive continuum.

Fig. 5.3

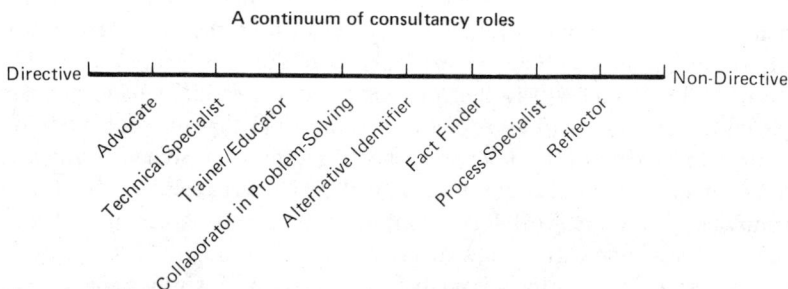

A continuum of consultancy roles

Directive ⟼————⊥————⊥————⊥————⊥————⊥————⊥————⊥————⊥———⟻ Non-Directive

Advocate · Technical Specialist · Trainer/Educator · Collaborator in Problem-Solving · Alternative Identifier · Fact Finder · Process Specialist · Reflector

SOURCE: Lippitt and Lippitt (1977), p. 136.

Some of the roles identified are fairly self-explanatory, such as those of 'fact finder' and 'reflector', but other roles are a little more obscure. They highlight the need for the consultant to have theoretical knowledge and practical experience of groupwork, to be knowledgeable about adolescent problems and reactions, and to have an understanding of the functions of intermediate treatment and of the organizational context in which it is located. It is also essential that the consultant has the trust of the social workers and that he is seen by them to be credible.

A consultancy contract should be formulated, taking into account the following questions:

Who has requested consultancy and why?
If the request has not come from the workers, what are their feelings about the involvement of a consultant?
What is the relationship between the consultancy process and the continuing process of line-management?
What are the limits of confidentiality?
What is to be the frequency, length, and venue for the consultancy meetings?

Below we outline three key areas in the work of a consultant:

Starting

The initial phase of a consultant meeting with consultees is a tenuous one for both parties. Therefore it is important to try and get these meetings right, for the consultant and the workers are exploring each other and trying to find the most productive level at which they can work. Where this might be a new experience for either or both then this process can prove far from easy. Initially the workers may hang back, expecting the consultant to give clear instructions as to what they should do. Alternatively, open hostility may be expressed about the involvement of an outsider, particularly where the consultant might start by challenging the basis on which a fledgling group is to be formed. Therefore having agreed a contract it could be helpful for the first session to be spent in exploratory exercises, perhaps by creating a framework within which workers and consultant can explore their expectations and anxieties about their sessions together.

Using Knowledge and Experience

Having stated that knowledge and experience are vital tools which the consultant should possess, it is also important to recognize that they constitute only part of the skills required. It is not uncommon to hear students say, 'He knows his subject well, but doesn't seem to have any idea of how to teach it'. The same problem applies to consultancy. Knowing what might happen in a group, and the different responses that workers can make, is only half the task. Being able to offer help to the workers in such a way that it can be listened to, understood, and then accepted so that it can be acted upon naturally, is the real skill in consultancy. The offering of knowledge, however, is not always a one-way process. If the groupworkers possess particular areas of expertise, then it is important for the consultant to recognize this, and to change his role to accommodate that knowledge. Failure to do so is likely to lead to unproductive conflict between the individuals concerned.

Recognizing the Group

Where a consultant meets with three or four workers who are running a group, then 'primary' and 'secondary' groupings are created. The primary group remains that of the adolescents, and this is the focus for the consultancy meeting. However, the consultancy sessions constitute the meeting of another group, which forms the secondary level. This secondary group is as likely to go through the stages of group development, or to experience issues over leadership, etc., as the adolescent group, only this time the consultant can become the worker and the workers the group members. It can then become difficult for the consultant to distinguish which group is being discussed. For example, an issue can develop between two of the leaders in the primary group. During the early stages of running a group it is common for leadership issues to be avoided, and therefore all the workers involved may avoid bringing this conflict into the open. There is then the possibility of this conflict being projected on to the adolescents, as if it is an issue between them, rather than being an issue between the two leaders. Although this might sound an extreme example, where workers are relatively inexperienced in an area of work it is often both difficult and painful to admit one's own shortcomings or failings and much easier to try and hide them. The task of the consultant is, therefore, to be critically constructive, supportive, and sensitive to those issues being presented. The objective test of the usefulness of the consultancy is whether in the end it enables the primary group to meet the goals for which it was created.

6. The Politics of Intermediate Treatment

In this concluding chapter we return to some of the themes that we introduced at the beginning of this book. In Chapter 1 we related intermediate treatment to changing social values and social policy, and to the arena of political debate. We now focus on some of the changes that have occurred since the implementation of the 1969 Children and Young Persons Act, and within this changing context we look at the financing, location, and potential of intermediate treatment.

Sentencing Trends in the 1970s

The 1969 Act was heralded as a major reforming measure within the field of child care and juvenile justice, but, as we have already noted, the Act was a watered-down version of the reforms advocated in the mid-sixties and it was further diluted by a failure to implement some of its most important reforming sections. Despite this, the Act has still been seen as a 'delinquents' charter', with the suggestion that it has not only failed to tackle delinquency, but that it has also encouraged some young people to become delinquent. In fact, if we look at what has been happening to young offenders since the implementation of the Act, we find that far from the seventies being a bonus for delinquents, it is more accurately characterized as a period of punishment and penal confinement.

✗Instead of the 1969 Act leading to an emphasis on the care and treatment of young offenders in the community, more juveniles are now locked up in detention centres, Borstals, and prisons than prior to its implementation, and proportionately fewer young offenders are receiving supervision orders. There has been a continued increase in the number of adolescents cautioned or found guilty of an indictable offence, but this is not particularly characteristic of the seventies as it merely continues a trend that was well established long before the introduction of the Act. Indeed in 1975 and 1976 there was a drop in the numbers of juveniles who were found guilty or cautioned for an indictable offence (we would not claim that this was a result of the Act beginning to 'bite' any more than we would accept that it was the Act which encouraged the continued rising trend in delinquency in the early 1970s). In Fig. 6.1 we record some of the changes in sentencing which have taken place since the 1969 Act was (partly) implemented in January 1971.

Fig. 6.1 emphasizes that the trend has been towards the punishment of young offenders, particularly by removing them from the community and placing them in custodial institutions run by the prison department. This trend is completely against the spirit of the Act and against the social values of the sixties which were reflected in it. However, this is not the result of hard-hearted magistrates overruling soft-hearted social workers, as the evidence suggests it is social workers who are recommending 'removal' and 'punishment-centred' sentences, and that it is their agencies which are failing to provide viable options to the locking-up of children and young people (see, for example, Thorpe, 1976). This is reflected in the increase in the number of children in the care of local authorities and the fact that when a child is received into care he now tends to stay there longer.

Fig. 6.1

Sentencing trends since the implementation of 1969 Children and Young Persons Act

ORIENTATION

		PUNISHMENT/RETRIBUTION	TREATMENT/ASSISTANCE
COMMUNITY	FINES	1970: 31.9%) 1977: 34.9%) + 3%	SUPERVISION ORDERS 1970: 24.6%) 1977: 17.8%) − 6.8%
	ATTENDANCE CENTRES	1970: 8.1%) 1977: 9.8%) + 1.7%	
RESIDENTIAL/CUSTODIAL	DETENTION CENTRES/ BORSTALS	1970: 3.6%) 1977: 7.2%) + 3.6%	CARE ORDERS 1970: 8.9%) 1977: 6.3%) − 2.6%

LOCATION

SOURCE: Based on Table 6.1, *Criminal Statistics for England and Wales, 1977* (H.M.S.O., 1978).

There is a suggestion that intermediate treatment itself may lead to young offenders being made the subject of a care order during a first appearance in court. This is seen to be a consequence of including 'at risk' adolescents in IT as an attempt to prevent them offending. When they do offend and appear in court intermediate treatment is already seen to have failed and the social worker recommends a care order. Thorpe (Draper, 1979) has concluded from this that IT should be available to those who are the subject of an intermediate treatment order, and that IT should be reserved purely as another step on the sentencing tariff. We disagree with this conclusion as we see intermediate treatment as concerned with tackling deprivation as well as delinquency, and we would respond to the suggestion that IT be reserved solely as a court disposal by asking four questions:

(a) Is intermediate treatment to be seen as primarily a penal measure, or is it a way of conceptualizing and planning a range of community-based social services for children and young people who may be delinquent, but who also may be *just* deprived or disturbed?

(b) If IT is basically a penal measure, then why is it primarily the responsibility of social workers?

(c) What happens to those adolescents who are deprived or distressed but who are not delinquent? Are they no longer the responsibility of social workers?

(d) If a social worker has contact with an adolescent who has offended, but who has not appeared in court, must that social worker argue for the youngster to be taken to court instead of including him in an intermediate treatment programme without the need for a stigmatizing court appearance and sentence?

The trend of social workers recommending to magistrates that adolescents be removed from the community and placed 'in care' following a first court appearance, or following a trivial offence, is not to be corrected by restricting the development of IT to just another step on the sentencing tariff. It is more likely to be corrected by resisting the swing of the pendulum where, in the late seventies, we focus again on the courts and the 'justice' of the law as the means of reacting to young offenders.

We should remember that most 'official' delinquents do grow up in deprived and disadvantaged circumstances. Where possible we should attempt to tackle that deprivation without waiting for the adolescent to prove that he 'deserves' our assistance by committing an offence. It seems unethical to have identified a need but not to respond to it just because the adolescent has not offended.

Yes, it *is* bad social work when children and young people are needlessly, and unjustly, received into care, but surely this should be tackled by:

(a) reallocating resources from residential provision so that care and supervision can be offered in the community,

(b) emphasizing, as Thorpe has stressed, the criteria which should be met before reception into care is recommended,

(c) offering social workers more support so that their tolerance of sometimes annoying and frustrating young people is increased, rather than allowing them to so easily 'reject' (this is the consumer's view) and 'regrade' (unsuitable for supervision in the community) their clients.

That social workers have not seized the opportunities to help young people in trouble is illustrated by two conversations overheard recently within one hour in a social services department:

(a) In the first conversation a senior social worker was telling a colleague that she was just off to a special hearing at the juvenile court. Three 15-year-old lads were to appear. They were being charged with criminal damage. The police would be recommending a remand in care. The senior social worker, however, was prepared to apply for certificates of unruliness, not because she considered that the lads were too unruly to be accommodated in a community home, but because she could not obtain any vacancies locally and saw it as a waste of social worker time to transport these lads to a home farther away!

(b) In the second conversation a supervisor was complaining that one of her social workers was intending to write in a social enquiry report that she would guarantee that a 13-year-old boy would be better supervised in the future during the early evening before his single-parent mother returned home from work. The supervisor argued that the social worker could not 'guarantee' this supervision, and that if this supervision was so essential to stop this boy offending then he ought to be received into care anyway!

There is a real dilemma for social workers in that caring for, and supervising, adolescents in the community requires an increased input of resources, and in the absence of a growing budget this means that resources will need to be transferred from other areas of work. In the above examples, for instance, it is cheaper for the social services department to allow the three 15-year-olds to be remanded to prison, and for the police to transport them, because the expenses involved then become the responsibility of other authorities – the police authority and the prison service. In the second example it is difficult for the social worker to 'guarantee' the supervision of the 13-year-old in the community while so much of her department's budget is committed to providing residential accommodation. The outcome is that the adolescent goes chasing the resources (he is received into care) rather than the resources being most appropriately made available for him (he receives adequate supervision in the community). The resources that are required to allow intermediate treatment to become a really viable option to residential care and penal confinement include money and manpower, although underlying these resources there needs to be a greater community commitment to befriend and tolerate sometimes annoying, but often deprived, young people.

Resources: Money

The provision of care and control in the community continues to be underfinanced in most local authorities. More (1978), in a survey of twenty-four local authorities, found great differences in the budgets for intermediate treatment:

IT Budget	Number of Local Authorities
£100 – £1,000	2
£1,000 – £5,000	4
£5,000 – £10,000	5
£10,000 – £50,000	9
£50,000 – £100,000	2
£1,000,000 plus	2

More's picture of the financing of intermediate treatment is supported by Tutt who, in a paper delivered to the National Intermediate Treatment Forum in April 1978, stated that:

> We look with great encouragement towards some authorities . . . who are putting large amounts of resources into a comprehensive package of services for young people in their area. Yet we recognise that there are not more than a dozen such authorities out of approximately 100 local authorities in England, and whereas some of this dozen may be spending something in the order of £100,000 on intermediate treatment, for every one there is another five authorities spending less than £1,000 on IT. (Tutt, 1978)

It is 'guestimated' that in 1977–8 the total expenditure on intermediate treatment was about £1.5 million (for 8,000 children) and that in 1978–9 this will have increased to about £3 million (for about 14,000 children), but when compared to the £25 million spent on keeping 6,000 children in community homes with education in 1977–8, then the money being made available for intermediate treatment remains very limited and the provision of IT continues to be at a low level.

Finance for intermediate treatment comes from several sources. Within local authority social services departments both IT budgets and section 1 (1963 Childrens and Young Persons Act) monies should be available for intermediate treatment, but in addition to local authority budgets, many voluntary social work agencies, such as the Church of England Children's Society, Save the Children Fund, and Dr Barnardo's, have made major commitments to intermediate treatment, and national and local trust funds have also provided finance. Central government has recently made available £200,000 a year (administered by the Rainer Foundation) for projects based on the services of volunteers, and urban-aid grants have provided a major source of finance for IT for many authorities. An interesting and informative account of the financing of one ROSLA project, which has hints to offer to those involved in intermediate treatment, is to be found in White and Brockington (1978).

But on what is the money that has been made available for intermediate treatment being spent? The following budget analysis (Salzedo, 1979) relates to one metropolitan district council's expenditure on IT. This authority is one of the few to have made a major commitment to inter-mediate treatment:

Intermediate Treatment Budget (March 1979)

Salaries – eleven area-based IT workers @ £4,150, plus £3,300 travelling expenses	£48,950
IT centre staff: one senior social worker, two social workers, one clerk	£17,070
Programme Running Costs – IT Centre	£6,250
Grant to IT centre run by voluntary agency	£9,000
All other projects	£3,520
Total IT Budget (which includes an urban-aid grant)	£85,060

This IT budget of one authority shows that the major expenditure relates to staff salaries. Fourteen fieldwork staff are employed full time on intermediate treatment, and other adult staffing for the projects includes a youth worker, a community worker, a teacher, probation officers, volunteers, students, and social workers (who are allowed time in lieu but do not receive sessional payments).

This metropolitan authority (population: 305,000) has about 150 children involved in intermediate treatment, and some of this involvement is quite intensive. A large county authority (population: 1,448,100) which has over 600 children involved in intermediate treatment employs twenty IT officers and has an annual budget of £63,000. It supplements the work of the intermediate treatment officers with 200 'IT aids'. These are volunteers who receive sessional payments for their involvement in intermediate treatment, and as with the metropolitan authority the experience of this county is that the main resource needed for IT is not money but labour:

> The amount of hours (the IT officers) work should be an area of concern for management. Fifty, sixty, seventy hours are common, especially through school holiday times. . . . The pressures of the job cannot be over-emphasised, the main problem being the constant anti-social hours. . . . Nearly all the workers are married and in some cases their family situations are coming under stress. (Moss, 1978)

Resources: Manpower

So how many workers are involved in intermediate treatment? A survey by the National Youth Bureau (1978) found that there were about 350 IT specialists in social services departments, and that 49 per cent of local authorities had an IT officer responsible for the development and co-ordination of intermediate treatment. The over-all variation between authorities was again highlighted by More's (1978) survey:

Number of Full and Part-time S.S.D. Personnel Involved in IT

lowest	1.00
mean	21.25
highest	136.00

A recent 'guestimate' is that there are approximately 1,400 full-time staff in intermediate treatment (Tutt, 1979), helping to provide IT provision for 14,000 children.

However, as the county authority above stresses, intermediate treatment is not, and never should be, just the responsibility of full-time specialist workers. Other social workers, other agencies, and volunteers are also required to give time and energy if difficult and deprived young people are to be assisted within the community, but in many areas the involvement of other agencies and of volunteers remains very limited, as More again shows:

Number of Local Authorities Involved in IT Programmes . . .

no other agency	8
1 other agency	3
2 " "	4
3 " "	6
4 " "	2
5 " "	0
6 " "	1

The general picture, therefore, of the development of intermediate treatment is that there are very large differences in provision between authorities; that some authorities have started to make a major commitment to intermediate treatment but many have not; and that although a good deal of progress has been made in the past few years IT still remains a Cinderella service provided for Cinderella children.

Positioning Intermediate Treatment

So far in this chapter we have attempted to give an up-to-date picture of the current state of intermediate treatment. Central to this picture has been the role of social services departments in the development (or non-development) of community-based social work services for adolescents and their families. But the picture is not as clear as it might seem, as you do not always get a full picture by just looking at numbers. Department A might have no IT workers and a low budget but a high level of volunteer and social worker commitment, with many interesting community-based schemes being developed; Department B, on the other hand, might have one expensive prestige project, and various central IT officers pushing paper and attending meetings. Department B has the visible (in terms of finance and manpower) commitment to intermediate treatment, but it is Department A which is really doing the work. Therefore the development of intermediate treatment can be furthered as much by the basic social work team having a commitment to involve the community, a genuine desire to work together, or a willingness to experiment with new ideas, as by greatly increasing finance and manpower resources. An argument often put forward during the early days of the development of New Careers in Britain was that 'more of the same did not always mean better'. Additional staff and extra money does not *automatically* mean better intermediate treatment, although clearly it should.

In Chapter 5 we commented on how difficult it is supporting specialist IT workers because of the number of areas that intermediate treatment practice covers. We also argue that intermediate treatment is in itself 'a challenge for change' by demanding the development of new ideas. It is from the juxtaposition of these two thoughts that intermediate treatment draws one of its major underlying themes: that of acting as a catalyst between existing resources. It can produce change by bringing together: education and social service departments to run joint day-care programmes; and the youth service and social services to promote community projects. Perhaps even more fundamental is that it can bring together social workers, often of different status levels, in running groups for their clients. All this 'bringing together' poses one fundamental dilemma – that of boundary crossing within a local authority system which is essentially constructed on a vertical/hierarchical model. It may be that residential workers and fieldworkers rarely meet because of this system, or that contact between teachers and social workers is limited because this is regarded as a policy matter between area officers and headteachers. For intermediate treatment two options become apparent: either departments accept that by encouraging its catalytic potential, IT may change the fundamental ways in which they operate, or that intermediate treatment may have to change to fit in with the existing system.

Option 1

If over a period of time several colleagues from the same team, possibly including a supervising senior or team leader, work together in running a group programme, then to do so successfully calls for close and sharing relationships between those workers. It is our impression that when this occurs many of the lessons learnt while 'working together' can start to have an impact far beyond the operation of the group. The basis of the relationship between supervisor and supervisee can change to a more open and honest level of sharing, and it can enable low-status workers, for example social work assistants or family aids, to feel of more value and therefore able to play a fuller part in the tasks of the social work team. Of even greater importance is that the whole concept of 'team' can change from an arbitrary gathering into a unified working group.

One of the authors, while working with a social work team that developed its groupwork with adolescents, was involved in such a process. Over a period of years the social workers began to set up groups in other client areas; staff turnover decreased; the team began to divide its tasks according to interest rather than status; client involvement in the department increased; and the amount of joint work, when social workers combined to assist families with serious problems, rose dramatically (Kerslake, 1977).

Option 2

When intermediate treatment attempts to dovetail with the existing system there are advantages as well as disadvantages. As we have argued, some tasks call for specialist workers and clear systems of support and accountability. Identifying and labelling areas of social work activity as intermediate treatment can help in the battle to attract resources (although it also means that those areas can be identified when cutbacks are demanded). Two problems in particular can arise when IT becomes a separate area of development. First, by creating a new specialization or area of work, the catalytic potential regarding existing areas of work can be lost. Secondly, departments have a tendency to become monolithic, and more concerned about self-perpetuation, than of achieving the goals for which they were created. A further effect of these specialist sections can be to alienate both generic social workers and other agencies, which in time can have an impact on areas as diverse as referrals and sentencing recommendations, with large groups of workers feeling superfluous to the development of intermediate treatment.

The positioning and development of intermediate treatment, therefore, needs to take into account three considerations:

(a) The concept of intermediate treatment requires the crossing of artificial boundaries within agencies.

(b) IT should be a force for change. Commitment to change has to allow for a degree of unpredictability, and as a consequence, developing IT may come to alter the delivery of social work services.

(c) Developing specialisms can have the effect of creating, rather than dissolving, boundaries.

Below we consider various tactics and strategies that can improve the breadth, depth, and performance of intermediate treatment.

Departmental Tactics

(a) We have laid heavy stress on the need to gain support from the social work team in promoting intermediate treatment. Support, however, does not simply occur by asking for it; it needs to be developed. In some areas the growth in intermediate treatment could be accounted for by the charisma of its IT officer. However, because charismatic IT officers tend to be one of the country's most mobile labour forces, and because the projects sometimes collapsed after they had left, the tactic of using charisma for promoting intermediate treatment can be seen to have limited mileage. An equally redundant strategy seems to be in confining the discussion and practice of intermediate treatment to the under-thirties age group. This is changing as the initial batches of IT workers get a little longer in the tooth, although hopefully the reason is that there has also been an increasing realization that it is not necessary to be Chris Bonington and Chay Blythe rolled into one (both of whom are over 30 anyway!) to become involved in intermediate treatment. So tactic one is: *Start from the basis that everyone in the social work team has a part to play in the development of intermediate treatment, and plan accordingly.*

(b) Social work to the outsider (and sometimes to the insider) often has the appearance of mystifying the ordinary. Terms and techniques, from transactional analysis to integrated methods, do not always have the same meaning to all, and to some might have no meaning at all (we even heard the other day of someone 'adumbrating the gestalt', whatever that means). If workers are being asked to follow or implement new techniques then it is essential that those who understand them explain clearly what they are, and lead by example. We have already mentioned how working in intermediate treatment groups can be stressful and demanding, particularly when undertaken for the first time. It might therefore be important for the experienced practitioner to lead and allow the uninitiated worker to follow at an easier pace. Tactic two is: *Offer support and leadership where appropriate and try not to avoid taking the initiative.*

(c) Most social work agencies are rife with administrative procedures and systems, many of them for good reason. To the social worker, and to the IT officer, these can appear time-consuming and unnecessary, but to ignore them means cutting off potential avenues for gaining resources. Funding can often be obtained by knowing the right time to apply for money. In January, departments are concerned about making sure that budgets have been spent so that the same amount can be obtained next year. Putting in claims for equipment at this time can often mean that money is transferred from an underused budget into those that need more.

As an area of work that lays stress on communicating, social work departments rarely practise what they preach, and every desk always seems to be littered with vast numbers of badly written, and hence largely unread, reports. The IT worker should know when it is important to get a written commitment as opposed to a comment during a telephone conversation – which is easier to retract. Policy statements that outline the future development of intermediate treatment should be encouraged, and of prime importance is the presentation of accurate, well-written and readable reports on projects which clearly discriminate between items for discussion and items for decision. Tactic three is: *Use existing systems. Do not make points of principle out of unimportant issues. Write reports so that people actually enjoy reading them.*

(d) Most social services departments have one of two organizational structures (see Brunel Institute of Organisational and Social Studies, 1974); they either have a centralized model with most of the power based at county hall, or a divisional model, with power decentralized to geographical districts normally covering two or three social work teams. For the area-based specialist and the generic social worker who wishes to influence the policy development of intermediate treatment, then the latter structure offers more possibilities. In the divisional system the control of residential, day care, and fieldwork resources is based locally, thereby making 'boundary crossing' that much easier. Decisions regarding the allocation of resources are also taken in the same office or building, which allows greater possibilities for personal influence. In the county-based structure, particularly in rural areas, the task is not so easy, because for manager and worker alike the opportunities for communication and influence are less. For those attempting to influence the development of intermediate treatment, it is important to work out how decisions are taken, who really holds the power, and what kind of IT programme is most likely to meet with approval. Promoting intermediate treatment does not mean using every available opportunity to talk about it: the process is far more subtle. Gaining team support and writing good reports

are two areas we have already discussed, but there are also other tactics. Making sure that management is well briefed about projects in operation, asking for them to be represented if visitors from outside agencies or educational establishments come to see the work you are doing, and offering well presented feedback from courses and conferences, are all methods by which the department becomes identified with intermediate treatment. So tactic four is: *Sort out the power structure and avenues of influence within the agency. But do not harp on one theme too much or IT will only succeed in getting identified as your special interest, rather than as a mainstream part of the department's work.*

Strategies for Developing Intermediate Treatment

In Chapter 5 (pp. 87-9) we described one exercise for an in-service training course, where the purpose was not to find the right solution to a problem but instead to generate ideas. This kind of task, often called brainstorming or lateral thinking, has a particular relevance to intermediate treatment. In the very first paragraph of this book we referred to the then Home Secretary talking about 'new flexible kinds of supervision which . . . can bring a new excitement into the way in which we treat young people'. However, intermediate treatment schemes still appear to cluster around the once-a-week activity group and the short-stay residential centre. By adopting a more flexible approach to our thinking, and then applying a greater degree of objectivity to our ideas, it may still be possible to reverse the trend of narrowing options. Strategies one and two below look at ways in which we can expand and broaden our thinking.

Strategy 1: Lateral Thinking

Edward de Bono, the main proponent of lateral thinking, states that:

> Since Aristotle, logical thinking has been exalted as the one effective way in which to use the mind. Yet the very elusiveness of new ideas indicates that they do not necessarily come about as a result of logical thinking processes. Some people are aware of another sort of thinking which is most easily recognised when it leads to those simple ideas that are obvious only after they have been thought of. (de Bono, 1971)

Lateral thinking is the phrase that has been coined to describe a process that is quite distinct from logic and is often more useful in the generation of ideas. We are all aware of how chance can play a major part in scientific discoveries – Fleming and penicillin, and Röntgen and X-rays, are just two examples. De Bono argues that rather than waiting for chance ideas to occur to us we can actively encourage their arrival. Associated with this is the idea that sometimes searching for an opposite or different line of thought can be of benefit.

There are four general principles which describe lateral thinking:

(a) Recognition of dominant polarizing ideas:

> It is not possible to dig a hole in a different place by digging the same hole deeper. Logic is the tool that is used to dig holes deeper and bigger, to make them altogether better holes. But if the hole is in the wrong place, then no amount of improvement is going to put it in the right place. No matter how obvious this may seem to every digger, it is still easier to go on digging in the same hole than to start all over again in a new place. Vertical thinking is digging the same hole deeper; lateral thinking is trying again elsewhere. (de Bono, 1971)

A good example of the dominance of existing ideas is in our present social security system. Most politicians accept that the present system (or hole) has got too cumbersome and complex, and yet so much is invested in its maintenance that it has become almost impossible to change it radically.

A similar problem can be observed in the development of intermediate treatment. The dominant polarizing ideas were those of one-to-one supervision and residential care, and therefore to succeeed IT needed to enter into battle with those concepts. Initially a considerable amount of money and effort was expended searching for a single answer to the question of 'What is IT?', instead of seeing it as a concept which became self-defined by virtue of practice. 'A dominant idea may be compared to a river that has cut deep into the land. The water which might have settled on the land is drained off so fast that there is no opportunity for lakes or other rivers to form' (de Bono, 1971).

(b) The search for different ways of looking at things:

Shifting the ways in which we look at a problem can often be of benefit. Jenner discovered vaccination by shifting his attention from why people got smallpox to why diarymaids did not. In criminology there has been a school of thought which has argued that we can learn more about adolescent crime by looking at those who, despite similar circumstances, do not commit offences as opposed to looking at those who do. Challenging well-established ideas is far from easy; there is often too much invested in them. The response is frequently that you have no right to challenge an old idea until you can come up with a better one. Separating the examination of ideas from searching for correct solutions can be a major stimulant to the discovery of new ideas.

(c)   A relaxation of the rigid control of vertical thinking:

> Stone by stone, a causeway is constructed by logic through the mud of unformed ideas. Each stone is firm and correctly placed. Indeed, each successive stone can be placed only if one is standing firmly on the one previously laid. With logical control it is necessary to be tight at every stage – that is the very essence of logic.
> But with lateral thinking it is not necessary to be right all the time. It is only the final conclusion that must be correct. Lateral thinking means getting down into the mud and searching around until a natural causeway is found. The need to be right at every stage and all the time is probably the biggest bar there is to new ideas. (de Bono, 1971)

(d)   The use of chance:

We have already mentioned how chance has played a major part in many scientific discoveries, often where years of logical research have produced few results. It is possible to encourage the use of chance by not automatically rejecting ideas which seem irrelevant. In writing it sometimes occurs that when looking for a reference you stumble across another article which is found to be more relevant. Automatic rejection of illogical or chance ideas can often inhibit our thinking rather than help it.

Table 6.1 offers three strategies by which the principles involved in lateral thinking may be put into practice, with particular relevance to intermediate treatment.

Having attempted to offer ways by which we can stimulate our thinking about intermediate treatment, it now becomes necessary to sort the ideas developed into a system of priorities. Defining priorities and setting objectives often seems to pose problems for workers involved in IT, probably once more because of the diversity of the task with which we are confronted.

Strategy 2: Objective Setting

Completing the objective setting exercise in Table 6.2 can hopefully assist the intermediate treatment worker, or indeed any social worker, to define priorities and set goals for the future. Although there is often a need, if not a requirement, to re-examine objectives frequently in the light of new information or experiences, the actual task of thinking about what you are doing, why, and in what order you wish to put those tasks, can be of obvious benefit (Ansoff, 1968). James puts forward some of the reasons for developing objective setting:

Table 6.1 Strategies for developing lateral thinking

Using an impossible idea as an intermediary to a potential solution	*How to use an intermediate impossible*
	1. Instead of rejecting an idea instantly, look at it a little longer and attempt to find good points that you might not have noticed had you rejected it straightaway.
	2. Judged within the framework of your current views on a subject the idea may be wrong. But if you hold on to the idea you might find that it is right, and that your current framework needs changing.
	3. The idea is definitely wrong, and always will be, yet it can still act as a stepping-stone to an idea that is appropriate.
	When to use an intermediate impossible
	1. In your own thinking, when you come to a wrong idea that you would normally discard immediately, protect the idea for a while and see if you can use it as a bridge to a new idea.
	2. When other people come to you with an idea that you could reject at once, instead listen and see if you can attempt to make that idea possible.
	3. You can deliberately set up an impossible solution to help in solving a problem that requires creativity.

In putting forward any new ideas to a social work team it is easy to get the impression that people become convinced that by rejecting the new idea it helps to validate the old. Intermediate treatment, by becoming involved in an ideological conflict with residential care, may miss several of its potential benefits. As an *exercise* it might be worth examining the possible impact of asking for no funding next year or constructing IT programmes without any groupwork!

Random juxtaposition	The purpose of random juxtaposition is to see what happens when two unrelated ideas are put together as an attempt to generate a new idea. For example:

The problem is to design a new type of confectionary. The random word is telephone. Not a very likely juxtaposition, it would seem, and yet it is possible to generate new ideas.

Telephones have dials so that you can ring who you want. What about dialled confectionary? For instance a coin operated machine in which you could dial different tastes and textures and the result

Table 6.1 continued

would come out as a sort of rope of intertwined strands. . . . Perhaps a candy which made noises or buzzed as you ate it, in order to provide more sensation. Perhaps a vibrating cigarette for those who wanted to give up smoking but still required oral stimulation. Telephone delays. A confectionary which delayed tastes so that the taste would change two or three times as you ate. A hand held device which squirted small jets of confectionary into your mouth. (de Bono, 1973)

Trying random juxtapositioning could be fun as well as potentially beneficial. Try combining words from these two groups:

(a)   Intensive projects, foster parents, weekly groups, truant schools,
(b)   Newspapers, pop music, warehouses, Red Indians, pubs.

Anti-rejection   The present thinking system often demands that you reject one idea before you can consider another. Anti-rejection is simply an invitation to generate alternative ways of looking at things. Three possible statements can be made that will help to avoid rejection:

1. 'That idea is O.K., but if we put it on one side for a minute we may find another way of looking at the problem.'
2. 'That answer is perfectly valid, but it does not exclude other possibilities, so let's try and find some.'
3. 'I wonder if there are any other possible ways of looking at this problem.'

Although the suggestions made above are fairly innocuous, they can still provoke an extreme reaction in many people. The domination of the vertical thinking system, particularly in meetings, can often mean that anyone who questions an answer that appears to be correct, or who suggests that, even though a satisfactory answer has been reached, there might be other choices, is likely to be viewed as obstructive, or as a trouble-maker. Therefore try it with care. Anti-rejection is, however, gaining some ground, as several recent publications on groupwork and social skills training have stressed an eclectic approach on the basis of 'if an idea works, use it; if not, remember it for another occasion'.

Management by Objectives is a system which can bring about many changes in organisations. It may be the means of effective 'planning from below' enabling the 'grassroots' practitioners in the organisation to make their full contribution to planning and policy formation. It may be the means of stimulating a significant organisational change, perhaps in the formal organisational structure, perhaps in the definition of individual or group roles. It may be the means of developing more effective methods of working, of more accurate definition of staffing standards, work standards and of the development needs of individuals and groups. It may stimulate heightened job satisfaction for employees and more active involvement in the work. Through the medium of action plans, improvement may be stimulated at the level of the department, as well as at the level of the individual manager. (James, 1976)

There are a few points that we should make about the exercise offered:

(a) Answering the questions to maximum effect can often only be achieved by another individual helping you to test out the reality of the answers that you have given. In many instances this might be a line manager, a supervisor, or a consultant. It could, however, be a group of colleagues, or members of an in-service training course.

(b) The results of the exercise should not become a blueprint which is followed regardless of the circumstances. Instead it should be a reference or background document which can be referred to when day-to-day issues cloud the objectives you are trying to achieve.

(c) A primary objective in completing the questions is to attempt to match your individual goals to those set by the agency, and to expose when they do not match. This is where completing the task with the involvement of a line manager is particularly useful.

(d) Although the decision you arrive at should not be seen as a rigid blueprint, it is important to check how far the key results have been achieved at the end of the specified time period. When doing this the reasons for both failure and success should be noted, and then taken into account when re-setting goals for the next period.

Conclusion

In this chapter we started by attempting to offer a picture of sentencing trends and the allocation of resources that have influenced the development of intermediate treatment. We followed this by examining how the positioning of IT within social services departments can affect its development. Finally, we have suggested some tactics and strategies that may be used on a local basis by those concerned to promote intermediate treatment. This follows the approach which we have adopted throughout the book of focusing on what workers in departments might be able to do,

Table 6.2   An objective setting exercise

Stages

1. *Define priority departmental effectiveness areas*

   List what you see as the five main areas in which your department could be most effective in the coming year.

2. *Define key departmental results*

   List what you see as specific key results, deadlines or targets which your department should have achieved by the end of the next six months within each of the five effectiveness areas listed above.

3. *Define priority personal effectiveness areas*

   List what you see as your own five main effectiveness areas in the coming year.

4. *Define key personal results*

   List what you see as your five specific key results, deadlines or targets which you should have achieved by the end of the next six months within each of the five personal effectivensss areas listed above.

5. *Define agency and staff blockages*

   List the five main blockages to your achieving your five key results and optimum effectiveness.

6. *Actions for improvement*

   List five practical, feasible steps you would like your agency to take which would help to increase effectiveness and the attainment of key results.

7. *Key personal tasks or activities*

   List what you see as the five specific key tasks or activities which will contribute most to your attainment of key results.

8. *Test out and evaluate your work in terms of 1–7 above*

SOURCE: Tony Scott, National Institute for Social Work.

as opposed to a detailed review of national developments and trends, or an examination of particular key projects.

In concluding we identify seven key points which we feel are crucial in considering and promoting the progress and development of intermediate treatment:

(a) In recent years there have been increasing demands to 'get tough with delinquents'. We reject this demand as there is no evidence that harsher, less humane sentencing leads to a reduction in offending, either

for the individual delinquent or for the over-all national picture. Disadvantaging the disadvantaged is not our aim, yet this seems to have been the effect of certain types of intervention, as with the old approved school system:

> The Approved School system is failing on three major counts and succeeding only unintentionally on a fourth. It is failing on the counts of custody, rehabilitation, and treatment, and succeeding on the count of punishment in so far as its effect on the client is detrimental. (Tutt, 1974)

(b) We would reiterate our perception of intermediate treatment as a conceptual term rather than as a description of a method of work. Although the *range* of projects nationally looks impressive, few authorities have as yet developed anything like a wide range of provision within any one area. The consequences of this can be to try to make projects achieve objectives of which they are plainly incapable because of inadequate staffing, little preparation, and low intensity of involvement with the adolescents.

(c) While there is a clear need in some areas of work for specialist workers, intermediate treatment needs to maintain a strong foothold in the social work team, otherwise there is the danger of:
(i) lessening the potential of IT to bring together areas of social work which are at present separated and unrelated,
(ii) losing the potential to influence decisions about reception into care.

(d) There is a need for IT to walk before it can run. Many conferences and meetings spend all their time discussing policy and definitions, when some of that time could possibly be spent more fruitfully in laying the foundations for good practice. Many groups, for example, still seem to start and operate haphazardly, with no clear ideas about objectives or how to measure if these objectives have been achieved.

(e) There is the possibility that IT could achieve the effect of more children and young people being received into care unnecessarily and unjustly. This could occur in two ways:
(i) As IT allows social workers to get to know their young clients better it could lead to the workers becoming more aware of the adolescent's difficulties and hence to more controlling sentencing recommendations.
(ii) A supervision order with an IT clause may be recommended because IT is anticipated to benefit the adolescent, although in other circumstances he may have received a 'lighter' sentence. Hence the adolescent is pushed farther along the tariff ladder. A consequence could be that when he next

appears in court he is sent to a detention centre or a Borstal, or he is made the subject of a care order.

If these dangers materialize they are the result of bad social work practice and are a reflection of the failure of individual social workers to argue persuasively for community-based sentences when advising magistrates. The dangers that we highlight above do not provide a reason for arguing that IT should *only* be available to offenders sentenced to intermediate treatment by the courts.

(f)   IT does have the potential to act as a diversion from residential provision. More resources need to be allocated to IT to explore this potential.

(g)   IT is not a solution to the problems of poverty, poor housing, unemployment, and meritocratic education, although for some individuals it could relieve a little of the pressure created by these ills.

References

1. What Is Intermediate Treatment?

Crossman, R. H. (1977), *The Diaries of a Cabinet Minister* (Hamish Hamilton–Jonathan Cape), vol. 3, p. 917.

Department of Health and Social Security (1972), *Intermediate Treatment*, Her Majesty's Stationery Office.

Hall, P. (1976), *Reforming the Welfare*, Heinemann.

Hansard (1969), Children and Young Persons Bill, cols 1176–1304, 11.3.69.

Hansard (1976), Eleventh Report of the Expenditure Committee, cols 1229–1337, 13.4.76.

Riley, J. S. (1974), Letter, *Social Worker and Community Care*, 18.4.74.

Sykes, G. M. and Matza, D. (1957), 'Techniques of Neutralization', *American Sociological Review, 22.*

2. A Framework for Planning Groups

Douglas, T. (1976), *Groupwork Practice*, Tavistock.

Hodge, J. (1977), 'Social Groupwork – Rules for Establishing the Group', *Social Work Today*, 8.17, 1.2.77.

Jones, R. (1979), *Fun and Therapy: Perceptions of Intermediate Treatment*, National Youth Bureau.

Personal Social Services Council (1977), 'Parameters of Groupwork Practice Related to Intermediate Treatment', in *A Future for Intermediate Treatment*, Personal Social Services Council.

Sarri and Galinsky, M. (1967), 'A Conceptual Framework for Group Development', in Vinter, R. D. (ed.), *Readings in Groupwork Practice*, Campus Publishers.

Smith, P. (1978), 'Groupwork as a Process of Social Influence', in McCaughan, N. (ed.), *Groupwork: Learning and Practice*, Allen & Unwin.

Social Work Service Development Group (1977), 'Notes on Groupwork', in *Intermediate Treatment – Planning for Action*, Department of Health and Social Security.

Tuckman, B. (1965), 'Some Stages of Development in Groups', *Psychological Bulletin*, 63.6.

Whittaker, K. (1970), 'Models of Group Development: Implications for Social Groupwork Practice', *Social Services Review*, 44.

3. Programme Planning

Brew, J. M. (1957), *Youth and Youth Groups*, Faber & Faber.
Button, L. (1974), *Developmental Group Work with Adolescents*, University of London Press.
Davies, B. and Gibson, A. (1967), *The Social Education of the Adolescent*, University of London Press.
Davies, M. (1977), *Support Systems in Social Work*, Routledge & Kegan Paul.
Morris, A. (1978), 'Diversion of Juvenile Offenders from the Criminal Justice System', in Tutt, N. (ed.), *Alternative Strategies for Coping with Crime*, Blackwell & Robertson.
Paley, J. and Thorpe, D. (1974), *Children: Handle With Care*, National Youth Bureau.
Personal Social Services Council (1977), *A Future for Intermediate Treatment*, Personal Social Services Council.
Pfeiffer, J. W. and Jones, J. E. (annual publication), *A Handbook of Structured Experiences for Human Relations Training*, University Associates.
Priestley, P., McGuire, J., Flegg, D., Hemsley, V. and Welham, D. (1978), *Social Skills and Personal Problem Solving*, Tavistock.
Raven, F. (1973), 'Admission and Discharge in an Adolescent Unit : a Case Study', *Social Work Today*, 4.4, 17.5.73.
Sainsbury, E. (1975), *Social Work with Families*, Routledge & Kegan Paul.
Truckle, B. and Schardt, E. (1975), 'Notes on a Counselling Group for Adolescents', *Group Analysis*, 8.2.
Truax, B. and Carkhuff, C. (1967), *Toward Effective Counselling and Psychotherapy: Training and Practice*, Aldine.
Waterhouse, J. (1978), 'Group Work in Intermediate Treatment', *British Journal of Social Work*, 8.2.
White, R. and Brockington, D. (1978), *In and Out of School*, Routledge & Kegan Paul.

4. Mobilizing Community and Neighbourhood Resources

Aves, G. M. (1969), *The Voluntary Worker in the Social Services*, Allen & Unwin.
Barr, H. (1971), *Volunteers in Probation After-care*, Allen & Unwin.
Holme, A. and Maizels, J. (1978), *Social Workers and Volunteers*, Allen & Unwin.
Jones, R. (1979), *Fun and Therapy: Perceptions of Intermediate Treatment*, National Youth Bureau.
Leissner, A., Powley, T. and Evans, D. (1977), *Intermediate Treatment*, National Children's Bureau.
National Association for the Care and Resettlement of Offenders (NACRO) (1978), *The Hammersmith Teenage Project*, Barry Rose.

5. Evaluation, Training and Staff Support

Allard, S. (1976), 'Intermediate Treatment: Slow Starter or Missed Opportunity', *Youth Social Work*, 3.4.
Herzberg, F. (1968), *Work and the Nature of Man*, Staples Press.
Jones, R. (1978), 'Intermediate Treatment and Adolescents' Perceptions of Social Workers', *British Journal of Social Work*, 8.4.
Jones, R. (1979), *Fun and Therapy: Perceptions of Intermediate Treatment*, National Youth Bureau.
Lippitt, R. and Lippitt, G. (1977), 'Consulting Process in Action', in Jones, J. and Pfeiffer, J., *The 1977 Handbook for Group Facilitators*, University Associates.
Millham, S. (1977), 'I.T. – Symbol or Solution' (Part I: IT and the Residential Tradition), *Youth in Society*, 26.
Warwick, J. (1977), 'Supervision and Intermediate Treatment – Staff Development and Training Implications', in *Aspects of Supervision and Intermediate Treatment*, Department of Health and Social Security.

6. The Politics of Intermediate Treatment

Ansoff, I. (1968), *Corporate Strategy*, Pelican.
Brunel Institute of Organisational and Social Studies (1974), *Social Services Departments*, Heinemann.
De Bono, E. (1971), *The Use of Lateral Thinking*, Pelican.
De Bono, E. (1973), *PO: Beyond Yes and No*, Pelican.
Draper, J. (1979), 'IT: An Offer He Ought to Refuse', *Community Care*, 19.4.79.
James, R. L. (1976), 'Management By Objectives', *Social Work Today*, 6.21, 22.1.76.
Kerslake, A. (1977), 'Maidenhead and Intermediate Treatment', in *Intermediate Treatment: 28 Choices*, Her Majesty's Stationery Office.
More, W. (1978), *IT: the National Picture?*, Priority Educational Programmes for Action and Research.
Moss, R. (1978), 'Intermediate Treatment in Kent', unpublished.
National Youth Bureau (1978), *Intermediate Treatment Mailing*, February.
Salzedo, S. (1979), personal communication.
Thorpe, D. (1976), 'Punishing Juveniles – Social Workers to Blame?', *Social Work Today*, 8.6, 9.11.76, p. 2.
Tutt, N. (1974), *Care or Custody*, Darton, Longman & Todd.
Tutt, N. (1978), 'IT: an Integrated Approach', unpublished paper presented to the National IT Forum, April 1978.
Tutt, N. (1979), personal communication.
White, R. and Brockington, D. (1978), *In and Out of School*, Routledge & Kegan Paul.

Index

Expenditure Committee of House of
Commons, 8

family
 involvement in IT, 15, 41, 62, 66, 71
  see also parents
 social work service, 3, 4

Galinsky, M., 36
generic workers, 92, 104
Gibson, A., 46
group(s), 10, 15, 16-38
 developmental stages, 36-7, 46-7, 56
 duration of, 29-30
 exercises, 46-55
 leadership, 21, 30-34, 57-9, 65
 models of, 24
 purpose, 19, 23, 25
 reasons for starting, 17-18
 recording, 22, 34-5
 selection, 21, 26-9, 31
 significant incidents checklist, 37
 size, 26-7
 venue, 30, 76-7

Hall, P., 4
Hammersmith Teenage Project, 75-6
Herzberg, F., 91
Hodge, J., 19
Holme, A., 73

ice-breaker exercises, 47-8
Ingleby Committee, 3
intensive IT, 11, 46, 60-66
IT in Action, DHSS (film), 49

James, R.L., 112
Jones, J.E., 48
Jones, R., 31, 67, 81, 91
Joseph, Sir Keith, 7-8
juvenile justice system, 11, 12
 adolescents' perceptions of, 50
 courts, 3, 41
  role play, 49-50
 and stigma, 99

Kahan, B., 4
Kerslake, A., 105

lateral thinking, 17, 108-12
leadership in groups, 21, 30-34, 57-9, 65
Leissner, A., 67, 69
life-task sharing, 52-3
Lippitt, R. and G., 94

magistrates, 5

advising, 116
 perceptions of delinquency causation,
  68
Maizels, J., 73
managers, 35
management by objectives, 110, 113-14
management system, 10, 17, 104-8
Matza, D., 13
Millham, S., 80
More, W., 100-1, 103
Morris, A., 43
Moss, R., 102

NACRO, 75-6
National Youth Bureau, 103
neighbourhood
 and delinquency, 14, 67-9
 focus for IT, 13, 68-9, 78
 friendship groups, 11, 71, 78
 resources, 11, 67-78
 see also community
Non-Residential Treatment of Offenders
 under 21, 3

Paley, J., 43, 62
parental care and supervision, 14, 40,
 41, 67-8, 71
parents, *see* family
peer group, 3, 10, 14, 39, 78
 and delinquency, 13-14, 67-8, 78
 relationships, 12, 18, 33, 45, 70
Personal Social Services Council, 19, 42,
 60-62
Pfeiffer, J.W., 48
police, 41, 72, 76, 78
politics
 agency, 103-8
 and delinquency, 3-5
 middle class youth, 2
Powley, T., 67, 69
practical skills for adolescents, 53-4
Priestley, P. (*et al.*), 55
probation
 officers, 10, 32-3, 102
 service, 9
 and volunteers, 73-4
programme(s)
 content, 42-55
 evaluation, 82-4
 intensive IT, 65-6
 planning, 39-66
psychosocial emphasis of social work, 15
punishment, 2, 7, 50, 98

questionnaires, 83-4